BUILDING COMMUNITY, KEEPING THE FAITH

BUILDING COMMUNITY, KEEPING THE FAITH

GERMAN CATHOLIC VERNACULAR ARCHITECTURE
IN A RURAL MINNESOTA PARISH

Fred W. Peterson

 MINNESOTA HISTORICAL SOCIETY PRESS
ST. PAUL

Title page: Frank and Elizabeth Deters farmhouse, ca. 1895.
Inset: Church of St. John the Baptist, Meire Grove, built 1885.

Minnesota Historical Society Press
St. Paul

Manufactured in the United States of America
10 9 8 7 6 5 4 3 2 1
International Standard Book Number   0-87351-368-1 (cloth)
                                         0-87351-369-x (paper)

∞ The paper used in this publication meets the minimum requirements of the American National Standard for Information Sciences— Permanence for Printed Library Materials, ANSI 739.48-1984.

Library of Congress Cataloging-in-Publication Data
  Peterson, Fred W.
    Building community, keeping the faith : German Catholic vernacular architecture in a rural Minnesota parish / Fred W. Peterson.
      p.   cm.
    Includes bibliographical references and index.
    ISBN 0-87351-368-1 (cloth : alk. paper). — ISBN 0-87351-369-x (pbk. : alk. paper)
    1. Brick houses—Minnesota—Meire Grove. 2. Architecture, Domestic—Minnesota—Meire Grove. 3. Vernacular architecture—Minnesota—Meire Grove. 4. Meire Grove (Minn.)—Buildings, structures, etc. 5. German-Americans—Minnesota—Meire Grove. I. Title.
NA7238.M45P48 1998
728' .6' 08931077647—dc21   98-38320
                                                     CIP

To my wife, Vasilikie Demos, who as a sociologist and colleague provided important perspectives, and who as a friend furthered the work.

CONTENTS

PREFACE AND ACKNOWLEDGMENTS

I began research and fieldwork for this book in 1988 while working on another book, *Homes in the Heartland* (1992). As I surveyed sections of Stearns County for that study of balloon-frame farmhouses in the Upper Midwest, I found houses that, while they seemed typical for the region, also appeared to possess particular German qualities I could not then explain. That hunch became stronger each time I viewed farmsteads in Stearns County, which I crossed frequently on drives from Morris, where I live, to Minneapolis. Traveling back roads to accomplish a thorough survey of the area, I eventually arrived at the village of Meire Grove, in whose vicinity are an exceptionally large number of farmhouses built with a characteristically German material: bricks.

Through the gracious cooperation of members of St. John the Baptist parish—of which Meire Grove forms the core—I located and photographed all of the area's existing distinctive brick homes and learned what I could about others like them that no longer stood. Because the houses were vernacular buildings, planned and constructed without the assistance of trained architects, no formal blueprints existed to facilitate my study. Thus I drew up my own measured floor plans and thereby increased, in a direct way, my grasp of the methods, traditions, and values that went into the making of these homes.

Yet at a certain point, after having collected a considerable amount of information about the architecture and history of the parish, I realized that the research resembled a complicated puzzle for which I had to find and position certain missing pieces if I hoped to form a clear and complete picture of what these German-American houses meant to the people who built them. I found those pieces scattered around the world—in Stearns County, in Minneapolis and St. Paul, in Iowa and Ohio, and in the provinces of northwestern Germany from which the parishioners' forebears had come. It became essential to understand the ethnic and religious traditions these people had experienced before coming to America. I had to learn how they built up Meire Grove and the surrounding farms. This involved focusing on all manner of details. I even had to calculate the dimensions of Imdieke bricks in order to learn how many of them it took to build a house. Now that the work is done, I believe I have joined the disparate puzzle pieces to produce a coherent, informed interpretation of the brick farmhouses in the physical and spiritual environment where they functioned as homes for the pious German-American Catholics of St. John the Baptist parish.

The process of reconstructing and interpreting the past confronts one with an array of challenges. In dealing with the challenges involved in preparing this book, I received support, advice, and direction from many quarters. First of all, I am grateful to everyone in the parish who opened their homes to me and responded thoughtfully to questions I asked about their families, farms, and houses. If it were not for Al and Sandra Imdieke, who welcomed me to their farm—which became my initial fieldwork site—I would have found it difficult to begin work in a rural neighborhood where I was an unknown. Dale Imdieke, whose farm is located in the village, became a steadfast ally, introducing me to other parishioners and scheduling fieldwork visits to various farms. I repeatedly visited Ann and Sylvester Nietfeld on their farm to borrow books on the history of the parish and to review information about houses that I had gathered. Recognition is also due to those who consented to participate in tape-recorded interview sessions, especially Walter and Marion Michels, who, during many years of friendship and one lengthy interview, vividly conveyed to this novice their firsthand knowledge of the cycles of labor and life on a Stearns County dairy farm.

A University of Minnesota Graduate School Summer Research grant, coupled with a matching award from the McKnight Foundation, enabled me to focus completely on the project for an extended period. I also benefited from a one-quarter leave from the University of Minnesota, Morris, during which I completed fieldwork in Stearns County and visited places in Germany where families in St. John the Baptist parish had originated. Funding for travel to Germany was provided by the university's Office of International Studies and through the Chancellor's Office at the Morris campus.

Colleagues in the Vernacular Architecture Forum—an interdisciplinary group that studies and promotes the many aspects of vernacular architecture and landscape in North America—supplied support and a professional context within which I could discuss my research and test my findings. I am especially grateful to David Murphy, Senior Research Architect, Nebraska State Historic Preservation Office, Lincoln, who encouraged me to persevere in the work. He provided many substantial suggestions through a critical reading of a late version of the manuscript. Jeanne Purdy, a professor of English at the University of Minnesota, Morris, reviewed the manuscript for organization and development of major concepts. Florence Meyer, a great-great-granddaughter of Elizabeth Meyer, the founding mother of the parish, also read a draft to correct names, dates, locations, and attributions.

At the Stearns County Historical Society, St. Cloud, assistant director of archives John Decker and archivist Robert Lommel provided me with numerous valuable primary materials about the county, the Diocese of St. Cloud, and the parish that were woven directly into this study. The finish and the polish of the text are the results of thorough efforts by Minnesota Historical Society Press editor Phil Freshman. He and other members of the press staff supplied the elements of support that brought the work to completion. Finally, Nora Koch accomplished the excellent design of the book. As a person of German heritage who grew up on a Wisconsin dairy farm, who is knowledgeable about architecture (especially floor plans), and who is a recent convert to Catholicism, she believed her participation was providential as well as professional.

Inquiry begins when an individual seeks answers to questions. Answers cannot be found unless many others cooperate with and contribute to the inquiry. The subject of this study is the building of a community. It is appropriate that many people, from a wide range of places and disciplines, became a community that facilitated the research, writing, and publication of this work.

INTRODUCTION

Only one hundred forty years ago, American migrants and
European immigrants began their struggle to establish themselves
on a frontier territory in the central part of the new state of
Minnesota. The area where they settled was at the eastern edge of
a prairie expanse that stretched west across the middle of the continent. Some of the migrants were Anglo-Americans from the
East, ultimately bound for the West, pursuing on their way entrepreneurial opportunities in business, trade, and land transaction.
Many of the immigrants came from German-speaking lands in
Northern Europe; they arrived with the intention of making a permanent home on the land through farming. They were willing to
work and endure in order to build secure households.

These immigrants carried what they could of their belongings on
board ship and train and on wagon or cart to places where they
occupied 160-acre sections of public land under the provisions of
the federal Preemption Act of 1841. They also, of course, brought
with them their language, beliefs, values, customs, and behaviors.
They effected a remarkable transfer of tradition to a new environment that modified but did not destroy their culture. Nothing so
firmly rooted in centuries of experience and the histories of their
institutions would vanish in the face of mere decades of challenge
and adaptation.

Through their religious worship they venerated saintly men and
women who lived two thousand years ago. They also observed rituals for planting and cultivation, instituted by the Catholic Church,
that had origins in ancient Greek rites performed to propitiate
Demeter and Dionysus. Their priest intoned the Latin of ancient
Rome as he led them in worship. The language they used in everyday life had its roots in the prehistoric speech of Northern
European tribal groups. As peasants from that land, they had

inherited strict rules and customs of village life and used those means to negotiate life between each other and with the land.

The village of Meire Grove and surrounding farms in four townships that comprise the Roman Catholic parish of St. John the Baptist in Stearns County, Minnesota, reflect the successful transfer of tradition from the Old World to the new one. Here, as members of the small parish, German-American farm families held on to significant aspects of their European peasant culture while adjusting to American society. Located in the Diocese of St. Cloud and surrounded by other communities of the same faith and similar ethnic composition, the parishioners remained insulated from many of the pressures and influences of the dominant Anglo-American culture. Cautious and frugal, they saw the old ways as the good ways and carried them on in building their community. They constructed their church near the center of the parish, in Meire Grove. They maintained their faith and practiced a piety inherited from generations of Catholic worship. They patterned their social life and structured their economic security on principles of discipline and persistent labor.

This volume examines the farmhouses and other salient structures of St. John the Baptist parish as revealing expressions of the German Catholic community that immigrants established there from the late 1850s through the early 1900s. While the book examines a particular community, it also provides a perspective on American life from the viewpoint of the immigrant families who built an agrarian-based parish.

The large brick houses on many of the dairy farms in the parish were distinctive features of the built environment that these pious German-Americans created. Supplied with materials from the Imdieke brick factory just north of Meire Grove and from a nearby lumberyard, local masons and carpenters fashioned houses that satisfied their occupants' preferences for strong, simple architectural forms that would provide enduring shelter not only for themselves but also for descendants who would maintain the farm in the family name.

This book is built layer upon layer, not unlike the courses that make up a brick wall, in order to convey an understanding of the vernacular architecture in the parish and the German-American culture that infused it with meaning. Chapter One presents a history of the parish from 1858, when the area was first settled, to 1915, when successful dairy farms had secured a reliable economic basis for the community and the last brick farmhouse was built there. This historical layer forms the basis for Chapter Two, which traces the making of log dwellings, the building of the parish church, the raising of large dairy barns, and the construction of substantial brick farmhouses. Experience and skill, tradition and innovation, labor and product overlapped and interrelated as builders erected these structures. The next layer of material, in Chapter Three, concerns the significant contributions made by the Imdieke brickyard, with an explanation of the brick-making process and the steps that craftsmen followed in constructing the farmhouses. Chapter Four documents and analyzes a representative sampling of brick farmhouses in order to show how various elements of their design and function reflect both national norms and the local German-American Catholic culture. Chapter Five carries the analysis one step further, assembling a profile of the community's social, ethnic, and religious values to postulate an aesthetic of vernacular architecture in St. John the Baptist parish.

In addition to perceiving their houses as beautiful, parishioners incorporated them into their devotional life. They believed that the spiritual power of the Catholic Church could be transferred to their houses and farms through the rituals their priests performed. Chapter Six considers the underlying religious aspects of the farm homes as essential to a full comprehension of their meaning. An interpretation of parish architecture on this level rests upon the previous "courses" of description, documentation, and analysis.

To form the layers of this study, and work them into a comprehensive whole, I collected relevant material from many areas. I consulted sources in national and international history, agricultural history, geography, rural sociology, and economics. My knowledge of art history and the history of both high-style and vernacular architecture gave me a familiarity with artistic currents and architectural styles that were favored by the people who made buildings on the American frontier between the 1860s and the early 1900s.

Research in regional and local history supplied me with details about the particular place and period. A published history of the parish, U.S. Census data from 1870, 1880, 1895, and 1905, plat maps of the four townships included in the parish dating from 1895 to 1920, aerial photographs of the area taken in 1936, and interviews with second- to fifth-generation parishioners offered an array of facts, assertions, ideas, images, and numbers that I checked for accuracy, analyzed, and interpreted in relation to the broader context of nineteenth-century European and American history.

Because St. John the Baptist parish was established as an ecclesiastical community, a domain of the Church, it was essential that I become familiar with the history, tenets, and liturgies of Catholicism. All parishioners who lived within sight of the church spire could draw strength from the traditions and authority of the faith. They experienced the nurturing presence of the Catholic Church through its sacraments and through the performance of sacramental rituals. Studying Catholicism supplied me with an abstract understanding of what members of the congregation of St. John the Baptist believed and experienced. And, because these people held to their faith in a particular time and place, it was beneficial for me to consult general sociological studies of religion as well as studies of German-American piety specific to Stearns County.

In addition, since my investigation focused on buildings that were functioning parts of farms and village, I relied upon the principles and methods of material-culture studies to guide my fieldwork in Stearns County, a "sister" German-American settlement in Iowa, and villages in northwestern Europe from which parishioners originated. Locating and classifying buildings, photographing structures, and making measured drawings of farmhouse floor plans and elevations were all vital in gathering accurate data on which to base my building analyses. An architectural-graphics computer program provided me with the means to generate clear, precise two-dimensional floor plans and elevations. The program also enabled me to create three-dimensional exterior and interior views from those plans; these furthered my understanding of how space, structure, and proportion operated in individual buildings.

I also drew upon various kinds of evidence—vintage photographs, interview material, and structural comparisons—to "reconstruct" some important buildings that no longer exist. The accuracy of these computer-aided reconstructions is, of course, open to discussion. A reconstruction of a given farmhouse verified itself when the plan and elevation displayed a consistent pattern of measurement and proportion—those logical qualities that are inherent in the structures and apparent in the skill and reason of the people who built them.

The numerous photographs, floor plans, elevations, and maps included in this study carry considerable information and should be seen as vital counterparts to the text. The reader's comprehension of the topic depends as much on examining the content of the images as it does on absorbing the meaning of the words.

Regardless of the quantity and kinds of historical material one collects, analyzes, and interprets for a study such as this, the treatment of the subject remains somewhat abstract. That is largely because, in producing the study, one seeks to delineate a relatively simple, abstract pattern that seems to characterize the life of a place—a pattern into which the various parts of the subject can appropriately fit. The pattern outlined in this book is not offered with the suggestion that people in St. John the Baptist parish enjoyed constant equilibrium and tranquility. Tragic events, disruptive actions, slanderous words, destructive dispositions intruded on their lives as they do on ours. Illness and epidemic, storms and drought, personal strife, accident, and death arrived randomly to fracture the pattern.

But a pattern was present, nonetheless. It was present in the path one always took from the house to the barn, in the recipes so familiar that they never had to be written down. It was present in the daily Rosary, the Sunday Mass, and the annual cycle of liturgical celebrations. Finally, it was present in the security promised, obtained, and tabulated in the labors of a good farm maintained in the family name. The patterns of life were safeguards against the potential disorders of human existence. Daily life in the parish provided farm families with a twofold covenant involving, on the one hand, the abrasive grit inherent in cultivating the earth; and on the other, the soothing grace of the Catholic Church, which gave strength and comfort in this life and carried the promise of a heavenly life to come.

Farm families and builders in St. John the Baptist parish had a high regard for historic record. Often, on finishing construction of a farmhouse, they would set a stone plaque, inscribed with the initials of the head of the family and the building's date, in the main facade. Completion of the structure was an event that marked both farm and family to that time and place. But such markings of significant events were not so much celebrations of something new as they were acts that perpetuated practices that had long since proven to be trustworthy and meaningful. If all the layers of the present study properly overlap and reasonably adhere to one another, then its title and date will signify the creation of something reliable. And the book will be seen as trustworthy and meaningful, its message as substantial as the structures it seeks to interpret.

I

I. GOOD WORKS AND GRACE

Herman and Henry Meyer,
ca. 1890

In June 1858, one month after Minnesota became a state, the brothers Herman and Henry Meyer arrived in Stearns County and claimed land. They each preempted 160 acres on gently rolling terrain that contained stands of hardwood trees, included a source of water, and opened toward a flat stretch of prairie that was suitable for cultivation. Herman was thirty-four, and Henry was twenty-three. As peasants in Holdorf, a village in the northwestern German province of Oldenburg, they had not possessed anything approaching this amount of land. On the east bank of a hill the brothers built a dugout that provided shelter for themselves and their widowed mother, Elizabeth. Shortly before their arrival, three other German-speaking immigrants had settled in the area: Henry and Xavier Schaefer and August Illies were all bachelors who, like the Meyers, had come from Oldenburg. They left the security of their families and villages, risking everything. They relied on their abilities to endure physically, adapt intelligently, and persevere morally as they strove to establish a kind of life on the Minnesota frontier that was different from the one they had left in Europe. These six individuals who stubbornly settled in to stay were the nucleus of a rural parish in which the village of Meire Grove became the site for the Church of St. John the Baptist.[1]

The people who founded and built this community were part of a global migration from Europe to the Americas that began in the seventeenth century and reached its peak in the late nineteenth century.[2] The Meyers, Schaefers, and August Illies participated in the massive social, political, and economic changes in the Western world that encouraged, and sometimes forced, groups and individuals to leave their homes and kin for difficult situations that threatened their lives, challenged their identities, and altered their values and traditional ways of life.

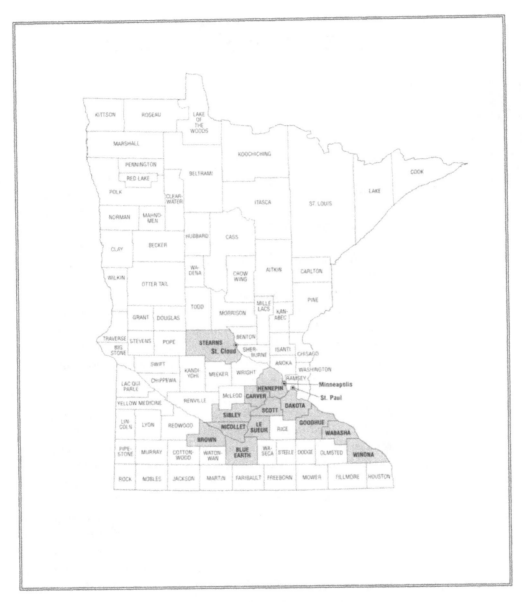

Figure 1:1
Areas of German-American settlement in Minnesota, ca. 1900

The first group of German-speaking immigrants to experience these kinds of challenges came to North America in 1683 after William Penn had convinced families of Quakers and Mennonites to leave Krefeld in Rhenish Prussia for the religious tolerance promised them in the territory that eventually became Pennsylvania. Religious faith and church affiliation continued to identify subsequent immigrant groups from German-speaking lands for some time. But in the nineteenth century, economic, political, and cultural issues emerged as the critical factors in emigration. During a period of political unrest that culminated in the revolutions of 1848, the numbers of European dissenters, freethinkers, and urban craftsmen leaving for America rose into the millions. Revolutionary manifestos helped spark unrest in many German-speaking lands, as they did across the Continent. The urban laboring class that emerged during the industrialization of Europe presented another unstable element in the cities of the German provinces. Agricultural reforms, rural population growth, scarcity of land, and loss of income due to the collapse of cottage industries were additional factors motivating many peasants to emigrate. Peasant families were drawn to America by the promise of good land and by the hope that there they would be secure and able to continue a way of life to which they were accustomed.

Between 1820 and 1900, approximately five million immigrants arrived in America from German-speaking lands. Although they spoke dialects of the same language, they represented a diversity of religious affiliations that included Catholics, Lutherans, and various sectarian groups. Further, they came from cities and villages practicing a full range of professions and trades.

German settlement in Minnesota Territory began in the early 1850s, along the Minnesota River in the newly formed Brown, Blue Earth, Nicollet, and Sibley Counties. Large numbers of Germans also settled along the Mississippi River, from Winona County northward to St. Paul. Hennepin, Carver, Scott, and Le Sueur Counties became the destinations for Germans traveling up the Minnesota River from the Mississippi or overland via St. Paul (fig. 1:1). The populations in these settlements, as in German-American enclaves elsewhere, represented a wide spectrum of religious faiths and political, social, and utopian credos.

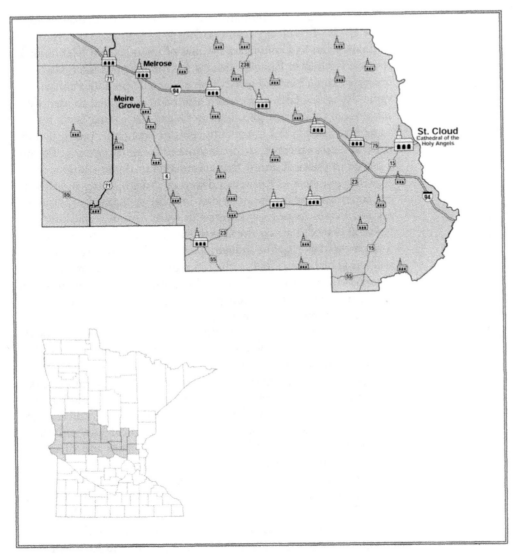

Figure 1:2
Left: Diocese of St. Cloud, ca. 1900
Above: Stearns County parish churches in
the Diocese of St. Cloud, ca. 1900. Sizes of
churches on map reflect relative sizes of
congregations and communities.

In 1849, the same year Congress created Minnesota Territory, a papal decree established the Diocese of St. Paul. Joseph Cretin was named the first bishop of the new ecclesiastical district. Under his guidance German Catholics formed parishes in Mankato, New Ulm, St. Peter, and in many smaller communities in the southern and eastern parts of the diocese.[3]

By the 1880s, Stearns County had the highest concentration of German Catholic settlement in central Minnesota (fig. 1:2). In 1889 Otto Zardetti became the first bishop of the Diocese of St. Cloud, an area of jurisdiction that included most of central Minnesota, including Stearns County, as its south-central focus. Those arriving here from established communities in the United States and from German-speaking lands alike responded to the Church's efforts to locate Catholics on suitable farmlands in the area. Father Franz Pierz, a Slovenian priest who arrived in the territory in 1852 as a missionary to the Indians, began encouraging German Catholics to settle in central Minnesota in 1854. In letters to *Wahrheitfreund* (Friend of the Truth), a German-Catholic newspaper in Cincinnati, he extolled the soils, the climate, and the abundance of timber, game, rivers, and lakes in that part of the territory. Determined to make Stearns County a German Catholic stronghold, he edited these letters in 1855—the year the county was established—into a tract aimed at spreading the word about the area to German settlers far and wide.[4] "It is my wish," he wrote:

> that the best and most beautiful localities of this most fertile territory would come into the hands of industrious Catholics; these settlers would make a Paradise on earth of a country on which God's blessings rest so bountifully; the boast would come true that the Germans are the most proficient farmers and the best Catholics. . . . Make haste, dear Germans, preceding all others, to pick the best places that are to be found in America for your settlement. You will certainly find the best land, the healthiest region, and all freedom, and you will be provided for spiritually."[5]

At Father Pierz's urging, the Bishop of St. Paul wrote to the German Fathers of the Benedictine Monastery at St. Vincent's,

Pennsylvania, asking that a delegation be sent to serve the spiritual needs of the fifty families who were then setting up homesteads along the Sauk River in Stearns County. Three Benedictine Fathers arrived in the Sauk River settlements of immigrant farm families in the spring of 1856 and, by the fall, formed three parishes. That same year, the Benedictine Fathers established the Abbey of St. Ludwig am See (later renamed St. John's Abbey) near St. Cloud. In 1857 a group of Benedictine Sisters arrived in the county from St. Mary's Convent in Elk County, Pennsylvania, to fill parish education needs and serve as nurses; they also founded a convent near St. Joseph.[6] This kind of ecclesiastical framework enabled pious Germans to create Catholic communities as they tended to their daily and seasonal labors. By the end of the century, the Diocese of St. Cloud numbered forty Church parishes in Stearns County.[7]

Father Pierz desired that each new colony be preserved as an exclusively German Catholic parish. He worried that German Catholic immigrants might lose the faith and traditions that had nurtured them if they were to live in places offering too much contact with people who held different beliefs and values. He advised immigrants "that . . . to prove yourselves good Catholics do not bring with you any free-thinkers, red republicans, atheists, or agitators."[8] An Austrian missionary society, the Leopoldine Foundation, was another colonizing agent of the Church; it foresaw a day when German Catholics would be completely insulated. An 1861 foundation report asserted that "Whoever wants to own land can chose here after his liking, particularly from the Yankees who all soon will move away from the Catholic environment, full of anger because they fear the sign of the cross." During the 1860s the Church erected a number of fourteen-foot-high mission crosses in the county. The inscription on the horizontal bar of each cross read, in German, "Blessed is he who perseveres to the end"—an encouragement to remain within the graces of the Church.[9] Not surprisingly, some non-Catholics took offense and began feeling hemmed in.

The Meyer brothers were among those guided to central Minnesota by the incentives and influence of the Catholic Church. Their father, John Henry Meyer, had left for America in about 1852. He worked in St. Louis to earn enough money for the passage of his wife, Elizabeth, and two sons but died before the money he sent reached them. Henry, the youngest, left for America in 1854. He settled first in New Vienna, Iowa, a German Catholic community that had been formed by the Church in 1843 with emigrants from the Meyers's home province of Oldenburg and peasants from the neighboring provinces of Westphalia and Bremen. By 1856 Herman and Elizabeth had joined Henry in New Vienna. But the scarcity and high price of good farmland in the area soon led the family to heed Father Pierz's call.[10]

The land the first settlers claimed provided them with a subsistence, and for the first two decades they led a hard existence as they worked to establish secure farmsteads. They had already experienced a regimen of farm work in Germany, but the new environment, with its particular potentials and difficulties, led them to learn new chores: clearing land, plowing virgin fields, and building shelters from locally available materials. The Federal Land Survey crew had just completed its work in the county when the Meyers arrived in mid-1858. Herman and Henry, the Schaefers, and August Illies were able to identify parcels of land on which they filed claims at $1.25 an acre, according to procedures and fees of preemption established by the federal government in 1841.[11]

Cultivating staples for the family larder began with the planting of potatoes and wheat. The pioneers fished, hunted game, and picked berries to round out their minimal diet. Trapping rabbits, mink, and raccoon and hunting bear for fur and skins provided some with a cash income. Others found work on large nearby Yankee farms or traveled back to New Vienna, Iowa, to earn wages. In the early years of settlement, anyone who was able to secure a team of oxen or horses and a dairy cow was considered wealthy.

Henry Meyer was the first of the bachelors to find a wife, marrying Elizabeth Schulte of New Vienna in 1863. Two years later, when the Schulte family staked claims in the Meire Grove area, Herman married Elizabeth's sister Bernadine.[12]

The labors of wives and children were essential in establishing and operating farms in the parish. A wife worked in the fields alongside her husband in addition to performing the many chores designated solely to her. The mother and teenage daughters were in charge of the family dairy cows. They milked the animals, churned the butter, cleaned the barn stalls, and fed the cattle. They also cared for the chickens and pigs that supplied staples for the table. They cultivated vegetables and fruit in the kitchen garden and were, of course, responsible for the preparation and preservation of food. When the men needed to leave the farm to take seasonal employment that would supplement the family income, the women took over and performed the entire range of farm and household chores.[13] Children, as soon as they were old enough, joined their parents in an agricultural venture that was, in the first stages of development, labor rich and cash poor. Father and son teamed up to coax and guide draft animals to plow furrows in the heavy soil. Breaking the plowed ridges of sod and earth with spade, hoe, and rake further tested their endurance. Then, using rhythmic gestures they had learned in the fields that surrounded their villages in Europe, the farmers broadcast the seed from hand to earth.

On average, an acre of land produced ten bushels of wheat. If each bushel sold for $1.50, a farmer could theoretically earn about $150 per ten-acre yield. A large percentage of the crop was, however, reserved to be milled as flour for the family's use. The size of the profit realized from whatever portion was sold depended on how individual buyers graded the grain and how much the farmer was charged for grain storage and shipment.[14] The level of profit a family realized in a given year was a measure of the pace at which its farm was developing into an economically viable enterprise. During the early years in St. John the Baptist parish, however, farmers worked mainly to survive.

It took a considerable amount of time and the labor of at least four people to harvest and process a crop from a ten-acre field for milling or market.[15] The men cut wheat and oats with a grain cradle and scythe, then bundled, tied, and stacked the crop in the fields to dry before hauling it by horse and wagon to the barn or threshing area. While one person opened the bundles on the threshing floor, two others beat or flayed the bundles to release the grain from the chaff. Others separated the grain from the straw with rakes and pitchforks. As one person held open a sack, another shoveled it full of grain. Another person stitched the tops of filled sacks shut before storage. The tools and toil required to realize any benefit from the earth were essentially the same as those demanded by traditional agriculture in the homeland.

Virtually every waking hour was devoted to tasks that would maintain life from season to season. The old German saying *Arbeit macht das Leben süsz* (Work makes life sweet) evokes the attitude parish farm families strove to observe as they cultivated the land and slowly developed their farmsteads.[16] They sought satisfaction in the labor itself, in doing tasks in a proper and thorough manner so as to ensure perpetuation of the farm and the family on the homeplace. Devotion to such goals necessitated long-term planning, a looking beyond daily and seasonal patterns of labor. Both imagination and will were required to project an image of how the farm should be in five years, in ten years. These families formed that image using the experiences and values they carried with them from Europe as well as the agricultural and building skills they acquired in America. The ideal they sought and the reality they achieved were also conditioned by external factors, ones that lay beyond their control.

National and local events during the 1860s and 1870s restrained the growth of the community. The Civil War brought immigration to a halt. In Minnesota, long-simmering tensions between whites and some Dakota Indians boiled over in August 1862, when the killing of four white settlers in Meeker County by Dakota men initiated the Dakota War. Confined to a reservation that had grown smaller and smaller, frustrated by nonpayment for land ceded by treaty, and suffering from corrupt Indian agency administration, many Dakota were eager to strike out against a people who, they believed, had robbed them of their land and deprived them of their dignity. While the war was primarily confined to southwestern Minnesota, it created panic among settlers throughout the state. News of the conflict pressured most people in the Meire Grove area to flee south to St. Joseph and St. Cloud. For months after the conflict ended, many prospective pioneers pictured central Minnesota as a dangerous place to start a homestead. But with the end of the Civil War in 1865, emigration from Europe resumed. The population of St. John the Baptist parish again began building with the arrival of families who had learned of Stearns County settlements through the established links of communication with villages and extended families in the homeland.

The parish economy was adversely effected by the depression that followed the Panic of September 1873; business closings and hard times for farmers prevailed across the nation through 1876. And, during the summers of 1876 and 1877 hordes of Rocky Mountain locusts, commonly known as grasshoppers, descended upon Stearns County, devouring every edible leaf, stem, and stalk in the fields. The insects also consumed clothing left out-of-doors and chewed into the wooden handles of farm tools, extracting the embedded salt from the laborers' sweat. These infestations were so devastating that, for many, hope of succeeding on the frontier disappeared. Many in the state abandoned their homesteads. Farmers who remained in St. John the Baptist parish dealt with the disaster either by pasturing their livestock in areas where grass remained or by temporarily giving up farming to seek wage labor outside the area. A chapel shrine built on the Carl Pfeffer farm in the summer of 1878 commemorated the end of the plague.[17]

Because of the poverty and periods of adversity faced by the early settlers, the parish economy did not demonstrate a sustained and substantial increase until the early 1880s. It was then that the efforts and endurance of the first generation were shown to have provided a sound basis for growth. During the second phase of parish development, from the 1880s to 1915, the sons and daughters of pioneer families built on the foundation their parents had laid and worked to maintain the material and spiritual well-being of the community.

Use of improved plows, mechanical planters, reapers, and harvesters alleviated the severity of farm labor. In 1878 two farmers, Herman Imdieke and John Primus, jointly purchased a horse-driven threshing machine that was used to process grain on many farms.[18] Markets for local grain crops opened starting in 1871, the year the St. Paul, Minneapolis and Manitoba Railroad reached nearby Melrose. The distance from parish farms to the grain elevator there averaged between five and fifteen miles. The road to Melrose from the Meire Grove area lay south and east of the Sauk River; thus the difficult and dangerous task of fording was made unnecessary. A round trip usually took one day.

While the cash they earned through grain sales enabled parish farmers to improve their lives and enter a modern agricultural economy, their inherently conservative outlook kept them from seeking to become the kinds of entrepreneurs who speculated in grain futures or developed large-scale operations. Moreover, by the mid-1880s, increasing numbers of farmers across the Upper Midwest were finally coming to the conclusion that raising wheat as a principal source of income was just too risky. Market prices for grain fluctuated from year to year as growing conditions remained unpredictable. Though the coming of the railroad was initially a boon to wheat growers, by the late 1870s, farmers in Stearns County, as in much of the Upper Midwest, were balking at the low per-bushel amounts paid by the grain elevators as well as at the high storage and freight rates charged by the elevators and rail-roads, respectively. Wherever possible, Upper Midwestern farmers began diversifying their operations by combining animal husbandry with the cultivation of a variety of crops, including corn and beans.

By the late 1880s, when daily sales of milk and butter became reliable sources of income, farmers in the parish began milking cows instead of growing wheat. This choice marked a return to something old rather than a venture into something new, for many of them had come from dairy-farming regions. The house-barns of their native provinces of Oldenburg, Westphalia, and Bremen shel-tered both family and livestock in close proximity. A family's status was judged by the size of its house-barn (*das Hallenhaus*) and by the number of livestock kept there. The temperament, values, and disciplined work habits of the German-American farmers predis-posed them to accept the exacting cycle of chores required to care for a herd of dairy cows—a regimented round of labor that demanded their presence on the farm every day of the year. Their willingness and ability to engage in this occupation were reinforced by the tenacity with which they pursued their goal of establishing an enduring home on the land.

The 1880s and 1890s brought additional incentives for dairying, including advances in knowledge about the breeding and nurturing of livestock and new means for processing milk and butter. Perhaps the most important invention was the cream separator, which was in use by many dairymen by the 1880s.[19] A new method of measuring the butterfat content of fresh milk, introduced by Stephen M. Babcock in 1891, permitted farmers to assess the quality of their product and its market value before they sold it at the local creamery. Also, it was found that more and better milk could be obtained from cows whose diets were carefully controlled.[20] In the area of veterinary medicine, a means of diagnosing bovine tuberculosis, discovered in 1882, enabled both farmers and government agencies to identify and eliminate infected cattle. This advance not only protected the consumer from that bacterial disease, but it also enhanced the dairy farmer's ability to raise and maintain healthy stock.[21] Over the course of a few years, a farmer could improve the performance of his herd by breeding only those cows that produced large quantities of high-quality milk. Some German-American farmers in Stearns County were slow to take up such breeding. They continued raising general-purpose cattle for use in hauling and for meat, milk, and hides. In Meire Grove, however, Herman S. Meyer, a son of the pioneer Henry Meyer, began in the early 1900s to breed full-blooded Holstein cattle.[22] The consequent improvement in his milk and cream production served as an incentive for other dairymen in the parish to obtain and nurture pedigreed cows.

The shift from wheat farming to dairying as the major enterprise on parish farms also brought about changes in domestic work patterns. For example, by the 1890s the men and boys of the family milked and cared for the cows, while the women washed the cream separator and cleaned the milk room.[23]

An unmistakable sign that dairy farming had become the basis of the local economy was the organization in 1897 of the Meire Grove Cooperative Dairy Association. This community effort, founded and administered by twelve parishioners, was part of a nationwide movement by farmers to control the production, transportation, and cost of butter.[24] The cooperative proved to be both advantageous for and satisfying to local dairymen, who, like other German-Americans, seemed to have a natural inclination to join mutual-aid organizations. The coop processed butter from the cream produced by local dairy herds. Coop members delivered tubs of butter to the Melrose railroad station, where depot workers loaded them onto refrigerator cars that transported the food to urban markets as distant as New York City. Standards and prices for butter rose as control of production improved and speed of transportation increased. A purer, fresher product reached consumers' tables. The Meire Grove cooperative won the prize for producing "Minnesota's best butter" at the 1908 State Fair.[25]

On a bright, chilly day in about 1900, the cooperative's members posed in front of the creamery for a photograph that emphatically reflects their sense of pride (fig. 1:3). In effect, the arrangement of people, objects, and gestures in the image comprises a *tableau vivant*, created to extol the organization's product. One wagon, entering from the far right, delivers cans of cream from parish farms, while another, loaded with tubs of butter, is set to leave for

Figure 1:3
Meire Grove Cooperative Dairy
Association, ca. 1900

Melrose. The gesture of the man near the coop's sign emphasizes the fact that the butter will be shipped to New York on the Chicago Great Western Railway. The test of quality occurs at center-stage, where a tub of butter has been opened for inspection. One can almost hear the exclamation, "Jawohl, das schmeckt sehr gut!" (Yes, indeed, that tastes good!), answered by a chorus of "Du hast rechts" (Right you are). The nation's flag flies atop the building. These were all good Germans, but they wanted to be identified as loyal Americans, too.

Meire Grove had become an official location on national and state maps shortly before the cooperative was formed; the village was incorporated and received an address in 1896. A post office, jail, schoolhouse, harness shop, two general stores, two blacksmith shops, two saloons, a few homes of village residents, and the Meyer and Imdieke farms were located along the dirt road that followed a north-south path through the village (fig. 1:4). According to the 1905 U.S. Census, farm families made up about 90 percent of the parish population inhabiting the village and the surrounding countryside.

Besides the working farmers, the community was comprised of several main groups. There was a set of skilled craftsmen who pursued agriculture but worked mainly as carpenters, bricklayers, laborers, and stonemasons. The village blacksmiths served farmers, as did the harness maker and farm-implement supplier. Elected dairy-coop officials ran that business and kept its records as well as paid bills and distributed profits. In addition, there were the merchants who operated the grocery and dry-goods stores and the tavern-keepers. The smallest but most influential group in the community, of course, included the parish priest and nuns.

The church directly contributed to the nature and quality of life in the parish.[26] The community began taking shape as an exclusively German Catholic one when the Benedictine Fathers started serving as priests, in the early 1860s. The first U.S. Census to include the county, taken in 1870, reflected the fact that the vast majority of landholders in the area were from German-speaking lands in Northern Europe. At this time, a few of the settlers in Grove, Getty, Spring Hill, and Lake George Townships had arrived from Scotland, Ireland, and England. A few Anglo-American families,

Figure 1:4
Oak Grove Street, Meire Grove, ca. 1900

who had come to the area in the 1860s from Vermont, New York, Virginia, Ohio, and Illinois, temporarily farmed land that eventually became the property of St. John the Baptist parishioners. U.S. Census data from 1895 and plat maps of 1896 indicate that, by that time, all lands in the parish were owned by German-Americans. Even a man named Michael Hanson, who farmed just southeast of Meire Grove, identified his place of birth as Prussia.

Parishes in the Diocese of St. Cloud formed when families and village groups journeyed and settled together to create a new community. Consequently, St. John the Baptist and other parishes identified themselves and became recognized by others according to the particular province in northwestern Europe from which its settlers had come. Austrians, specifically Krainers, settled in Krain and Brockway Townships. The villagers and farm families in St. Martin Township came from Rhenish Prussia. Bavarians

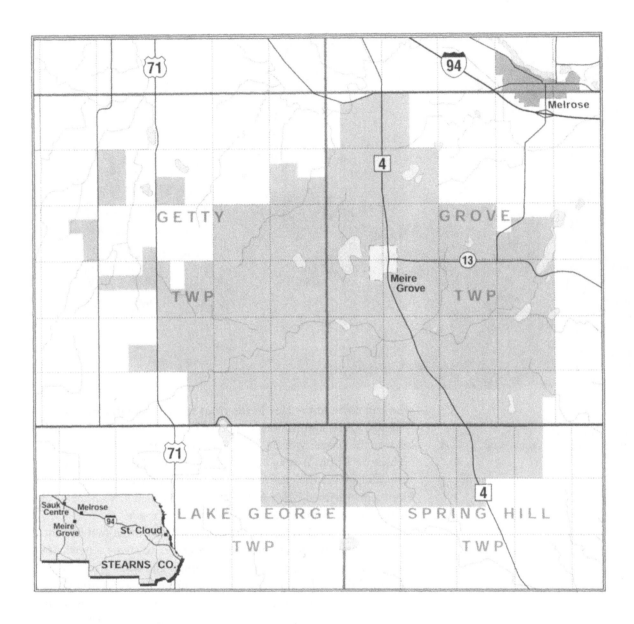

Figure 1:5
St. John the Baptist parish, 1896

clustered in Albany Township. St. John the Baptist parishioners cultivated a belief that they originated from Oldenburg.[27]

Approximately one hundred farm and village families lived within four miles of the church that was located at the center of the village (fig. 1:5). One parish history described Meire Grove in 1900 as "an isolated community in the German enclave of Stearns County. . . . Farm life [there], though gradually mechanized, changed little from day to day, year to year. . . . The quiet life of a rural parish steeped in its German heritage often seemed remote from the throbbing pulse of the nation."[28]

A fuller characterization of the "quiet life" of the rural parish at the turn of the century would note certain pervasive and significant traits and behaviors. These would include community members' continued use of the German language; their maintenance of the social structure they had known in Europe; the importance of the Catholic faith in their lives; and their conservative approach to both agriculture and landownership.

There were economic and civic incentives for immigrants to learn and use English, but in most situations within the insulated parish of St. John the Baptist people spoke German. Parishioners likely would have agreed with the reasons for preserving the language given by the author of an immigrant handbook published in 1829:

Germans, do not contaminate yourselves! Germans remain German! You will live through your language: Language will hold you stead-fast; solely honor and love it intimately! No one can replace that which is yours. Only the native tongue truly illustrates what the soul senses, thinks, feels and seeks. Hold this within you as a mirror of the people, so external forces will not rob nor will they undermine the unity of the people and the language.[29]

Loss of language, in other words, would result in loss of the habitual ways in which one thought and structured one's speech. Using the language of the homeland was a vital means of prolonging contact with its nourishing traditions as well as of helping sustain a sense of meaning and purpose in the face of challenges brought by life in the New World.[30]

Parishioners did not experience the socioeconomic hierarchies of rural society that were established in some areas of the Upper Midwest in the second half of the nineteenth century. The system of the large landowner, country squire, or gentleman farmer did not exist in the townships of Stearns County. There were no "dirt farmers" in the parishes who were transitory tenants. While some young men identified themselves as "farm laborers" on local township census lists, they were in fact earning wages that would eventually enable them to be landholders.[31] And while at one time there was a spot in Meire Grove referred to as *die smarte Ecke* (the smart corner), this characterization referred neither to snobbishness nor style but rather to the place where farmers weighed their cattle before taking them to Melrose in order to be certain of receiving fair treatment in the marketplace.[32]

The kinds and frequency of social contacts in the parish originated within the religious activities and duties of immediate and extended families. Marriages extended and strengthened the community's network of relationships. Sponsoring an infant as a godparent at a baptism, standing up for a bride or groom at a wedding, or serving as pallbearer at a funeral were social-religious tasks that further bonded individuals and groups. Church groups and organizations provided additional means for parishioners to meet in an environment that merged the secular and sacred aspects of human relationships. Village organizations such as the Meire Grove band and the local shooting club were reserved for male camaraderie. The band performed in secular events such as Fourth of July parades but more frequently led congregational processions during religious holidays.[33]

Virtually all parish residents were members of the Church of St. John the Baptist. As pious Catholics, they assented to the teachings of the Church and participated in the means of grace by receiving the sacraments and worshiping together. As spiritual father, the priest led his congregation in matters of faith and also in the many concerns of this life; canon law accorded him a wide-ranging authority. Members of the laity could also be vested—temporarily—with power in congregational and parish affairs by serving as trustees or officers of church-based social organizations.

Parishioners also used the ability to attain economic security for one's family, successful farm management, and length of tenure on the land or in the community as important criteria to judge position in the community. His status in the parish was assessed according to how financially secure he had made his family, how successfully he managed his farm, and how long he had worked his land. He might also be judged by the amount of schooling he had had, with a premium placed on agricultural education that was applicable to local farming. Holding the office of mayor or serving as a member of the village council were other means of attaining community status and influence.[34]

Ownership of land was of fundamental importance to parish farmers.[35] Like other immigrants to America, they labored to pay for preempted acres or, after 1862, to prove up a homestead claim. But, perhaps more than individuals from other ethnic groups, each conceived of the land as a place on which to establish the family name. They saw the farm as an enterprise that would support family members from generation to generation. Within one generation, the Leopoldine Foundation's 1861 prophecy that Yankees would flee Stearns County and that German Catholic settlers would predominate was fulfilled.[36] Approximately one-fourth of the farmland in the parish that changed hands during the first three decades of settlement was acquired from earlier claimants by German fathers seeking either to enlarge their holdings or to establish their sons on nearby farms. Land initially held by German-American families remained in the family name.[37] Henry Meyer originally preempted 160 acres and, by the 1890s, increased his holdings to 450 acres. Portions of that rather large amount of land were, however, signed over to Henry's sons when they married and began building households of their own.[38]

Following conservative methods of agriculture on a relatively small tract of land, the German-American farmer also preserved customary patterns of life at home. In the household, he held a patriarchal authority parallel to that of the parish priest. The family he directed and cared for typically included between five and twelve children. Children received a basic education in the township's public schools, but their primary focus was on the family farm and the chores for which they were responsible.[39]

These pioneers earned a reputation as industrious, frugal, skilled farmers who perpetuated a conservative life in their rural enclave. German immigrants to America have been generally characterized as coming "less to build something new than to regain and conserve something old . . . to till new fields and to find new customers, true enough, but ultimately to keep the way of life they were used to."[40]

St. John the Baptist parishioners were determined that their community would remain small and that they would retain control over traditional ways of life in the parish.

In 1907 the Soo Line railroad bid to build a track through Meire Grove. The consensus of parishioners was that trains would not necessarily improve their lives, and so they denied railroad officials the opportunity to purchase a right-of-way.[41] At that time, virtually any other rural community would have enthusiastically welcomed the railroad as an instrument of growth, change, economic prosperity, communication, status, and modernity. The village's decision was ultimately and firmly conservative in nature—conservative in the sense that the choice went against a belief in progress then prevalent in American society but conservative, too, with respect to preserving what was locally considered to be a good life in a manageable environment.

The folk culture of St. John the Baptist parish was at once so immediate and so deeply embedded that parishioners did not consciously recognize its formative power, presence, and vitality. They were not closed to new options, when they arose, as viable means to secure their farms and the community. They did, however, concentrate on the best assurances of establishing what they saw as a good life. The elements at the core of that life were a substantial house, a stable household economy, a patriarchal domestic order, and the shared religious faith and rituals that suffused every aspect of their experience. This was the way it was and had always been. A Minnesota writer, Herbert Krause, observed that the tenacious culture of German-American farmers had its origins in "something . . . that had no beginning in his memory but broke from bone depth and innate stirrings and the slow accumulation of the folk mind."[42]

Firmly rooted within a traditionally oriented community, tenured on the land, and secure after building a strong agricultural foundation, St. John the Baptist parishioners had by the end of the nineteenth century created an environment that satisfied their requirements for a sense of well-being. The structures of this "isolated community in the German enclave of Stearns County" included its church, situated at the center of the parish; its civic institutions and businesses, located along the village thoroughfare; its township schools; and its dairy farms. Erected by parishioners to protect them from the environment, to serve their social and economic purposes, and to afford them a place of worship, these buildings communicated qualities of simplicity and stability that arose from the "bone depth" of German Catholic folk culture.

II

II. STRUCTURES FOR WORK AND WORSHIP

Holstein dairy cows, Meire Grove

The farmers and craftsmen of St. John the Baptist parish built structures using resources in their immediate environment. Early on, they cut down hardwood trees that grew on their claims to form logs and planks for their cabins. Later, they used locally milled lumber to frame houses and barns. Ultimately, they raised brick and mortar walls for their church and their farm homes. During periods of growth and change the types of structures built—cabins and houses, general stores and blacksmith shops, village hall, schoolhouses, and churches—helped identify the community as a distinctively German-American one. In every structure they built, parishioners accommodated their aesthetic preferences and traditional ways of doing things to the necessities and possibilities of the new environment as well as to the influences and models of the dominant Anglo-American culture.

During their first months in Stearns County, the settlers lived in dugout shelters that protected them from the elements as they got their footing on the land (fig. 2:1).[1] Henry and Herman Meyer excavated a cavelike recess in a rise of earth that ran north and south through their claim. They extended the crude walls of the shelter beyond the interior by setting a row of logs vertically in the ground and spanning them with available materials such as branches, thatch made from meadow grass, or boards; in some cases, they obtained boards by dismantling the wagons that had carried these pioneers to the frontier. The dugout door was part of this small extension and swung inward, enabling them to enter and exit whenever the shelter was buried in snow.[2] As soon as a settler was able to build a cabin—usually within a year—this primitive shelter became a stable for animals.

Either a dugout or a cabin fulfilled the requirement of the 1841 Preemption Act that a dwelling be constructed on a claim during the first year of occupancy. The act of filing a preemption claim meant that the settler was identifying himself as the prospective owner of a 160-acre parcel of land. Filing drew the immigrant into a sphere of activity that was significantly different from the one in which village agriculture in the northwestern German provinces was practiced.

In many villages of that region, one heir received the landholdings of the parents and agreed to care for them after their retirement from farming. Sometimes parents could provide for other children when, in periods of economic well-being, additional land could be secured. Some children received no inheritance. They moved to localities where they could find employment or marry someone who owned land. In every case, holdings were small, dispersed parcels of land located in the vicinity of the village.

The physical qualities of the preemption-claim land and the building materials available on it challenged the acquired skills that had guided and informed the peasant in his work. In central Minnesota, he would learn to survive and succeed by cultivating unfamiliar land and by planting and harvesting in the prairie climate. He would strive to act as a moderator between tradition and necessity, between the old ways and new ones.

Written and visual evidence indicates that the settlers' log cabins embodied this cultural interplay (fig. 2:2).[3] The experience of building with wood that the Meyers, Schaefers, and others brought with them from the homeland enabled them to conceive of and realize these early dwellings with some skill and finish. The features of a Meire Grove log shelter were similar to a type identified as a German single-pen cabin.[4] Using a broadaxe, the builder cut the logs' interior and exterior surfaces flat before forming a half-dovetail notch at the ends and setting them in place to make the walls. In a similar manner, the builder formed broad puncheon boards for the floor and loft. He then gabled the upper portions of the side walls and covered them with vertical board-and-batten.

Henry Meyer was sufficiently skilled to make wooden hinges for the single door of his cabin and to split wooden shingles for its

Figure 2:1
Cross section, dugout subsistence shelter

Figure 2:2
Unidentified settler's log cabin,
Meire Grove, built ca. 1859

roof.[5] The door swung into the cabin's 16-by-20-foot interior, which was illuminated by one or two glazed windows and centered on an iron range that was connected either to a stovepipe or chimney. During cold months, the range heated the lower floor and took the chill from the sleeping loft. Its firebox, however, had to be frequently filled with fuel in order to keep the small cabin adequately warm. Although it was not the central fireplace—the traditional *Herdfeuer* of their dwellings in Oldenburg—this modern American appliance served as the hearth for the new home in Minnesota. The cabin was also furnished with a handmade table and stools and equipped with some utensils, iron pots, and plates. Mattresses stuffed with prairie grass or straw, spread out on the floor and loft, gave some comfort for sleep.[6] Though the cabin was small and cramped, the undifferentiated nature of space in it may have reminded these pioneers of the multipurpose kitchen area of the northwestern German *Hallenhaus,* or house-barn (fig. 4:10). Likewise, the small enclosed space of the sleeping loft, tucked under the sloping roof, was not much different from the *Bettkästen* alcoves (bunks) of the house-barns (fig. 2:3).

Joseph Zenzen emigrated from Germany in 1868 and homesteaded 160 acres in Lake George Township. His family's first shelter was a substantial log cabin measuring approximately 18 by 24 feet. In a photograph taken in about 1890, the original structure is visible as the larger unit behind the kitchen-wing addition (fig. 2:4a). The floor plan of the Zenzens' dwelling provides the earliest evidence of a division and use of interior space that immigrants transferred directly from the northwestern German provinces to

Figure 2:3
Bettkästen *alcoves (bunks), Gulfhaus, Cloppenburg, Germany*

Figure 2:4a
Joseph and Maria Zenzen family and
farmhouse, Lake George Township,
ca. 1890

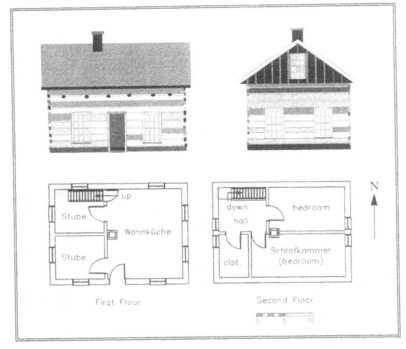

Figure 2:4b
Floor plan and elevations, Zenzen log house, built ca. 1870

First Floor

Second Floor

N

0 5 10

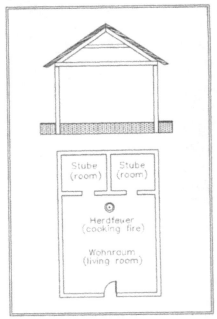

Figure 2:5
Cross section and floor plan, Niedersachsen Pfostenwohnhaus, 12th-century

the Minnesota frontier (fig. 2:4b).[7] The layout of the first floor, which includes a *Wohnküche* (all-purpose kitchen), central chimney, and two symmetrical *Stuben* (rooms) behind the hearth, derives from the Niedersachsen *Pfostenwohnhaus*—a folk design dating to the early-medieval period that included a multipurpose room and two subordinate spaces for sleeping and/or storage (fig. 2:5).[8] Like other settlers in the parish, Zenzen conceived of shelter in traditional terms.

The trees that provided logs for the cabin also supplied lumber for furniture, materials for farm structures, and firewood. Simple hand tools and implements facilitated the heavy labor of frontier farming. With a broadaxe, hatchet, wood plane, and auger the farmer-craftsman cut and joined wooden members of buildings, furniture, and fences. While most settlers performed much of the work to develop the farmstead out-of-doors or in primitive lean-to shelters, some used their small log houses as workshops. Imagination and initiative

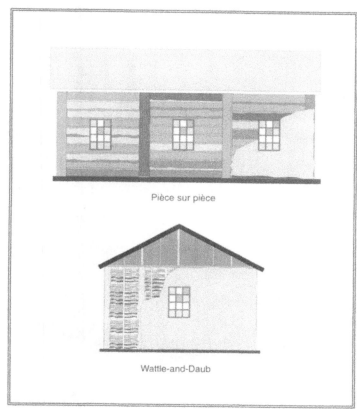

Figure 2:6
Techniques used in constructing
Meire Grove log church, 1864

Pièce sur pièce

Wattle-and-Daub

inevitably modified, but did not replace, accustomed ways of doing things. A make-do approach that involved both getting along and getting ahead reinforced the settlers' caution and frugality.

The earliest claims in the settlement clustered along the western edge of Grove Township, close to a road that later became the main street of Meire Grove. Near this road, on Henry Meyer's tract, parishioners built a log church in 1864 to house their small congregation, which was now served by a Benedictine priest who traveled through the area, offering the Mass at various settlements at monthly intervals. The church, which measured 18 by 30 feet, had a dirt floor and was unheated. Worshipers stood before a simple altar during the celebration of the Mass and other sacraments.[9] The interior is described in a published history of the parish:

Log posts set vertically in the ground framed the church. In between the posts, other logs, each tightly wrapped with hay, were laid horizontally one on top of the other to form the walls. A wooden shingle roof enclosed the church and a loam mixture was smeared over the hay-wrapped logs to close the chinks . . . and the log walls were plastered over with a smooth surface of loam.[10]

Because there are no images of the structure, it is only possible to conjecture about how it was erected. The brief description above suggests that Meire Grove builders used the French-American *pièce sur pièce* technique (fig. 2:6, top). Given the short length of logs that could be produced from local timber, this method, which permits the extension of a wall by adding section to section *(pièce sur pièce)*, could have been a practical way to build the church.[11] It is also possible that the builders relied upon construction methods from their native region. The medieval *Pfostenwohnhaus* consisted of a series of vertical posts set in the ground, with wattle-and-daub used to fill intervening spaces (fig. 2:6, bottom). The characteristic *eine Blockhütte* (log cabin) of the northwestern German provinces is built of slender tree trunks and stout branches. These members are held together by vertical posts that are set at intervals in the exterior walls. Considering how strongly the influence of traditional techniques is manifested in buildings in the parish—not to mention how recently the parishioners had arrived from their homeland—it is quite possible that this first church was built using a time-honored technique such as the one just noted.[12]

A program to school the parish children began soon after the church was completed. The Benedictine priest who served the congregation virtually required parents to bring their children to services on Sundays and holy days so they could receive lessons in reading, writing, arithmetic, and the catechism in the presence of their families. The success of this approach at winning the moral and financial support of families became evident when parishioners formed the first district school in 1865.[13] In this log structure and the frame schoolhouses that succeeded it, the three Rs of education increased to include a fourth: religion. Teachers at these one-room schools were young men, usually from the parish, who had obtained seminary training in the fundamentals of primary education and the

Figure 2:7a
Church of St. John the Baptist,
Meire Grove, built 1871

Catholic faith. The parish priest selected them as well as supervised and coached their work. All instruction was conducted in German.[14] Public and parochial education and ethnic traditions became blended in this rural "public school" curriculum, which reinforced the socio-religious values and habits practiced at work and at home.[15]

By 1871 St. John the Baptist parish had grown to fifty families, or about four hundred people. The log church was now inadequate, and the Reverend Frauendorfer, who was in charge of the Sauk Valley missions, proposed replacing it. The building of a new frame church offered local craftsmen their first large-scale construction project.[16] The structure measured 36 by 60 feet and had a bell tower and spire that rose almost 60 feet (figs. 2:7a, 2:7b).[17] The scale and complexity of the project required careful planning and coordinated labor, as compared with the makeshift efforts that had earlier sufficed. No local supply of building materials was adequate to the task. Lumber, nails, sheathing, and roofing materials had to be hauled from the recently opened railroad station in Melrose, six

Figure 2:7b
Reconstruction of floor plan, Church of
St. John the Baptist, built 1871

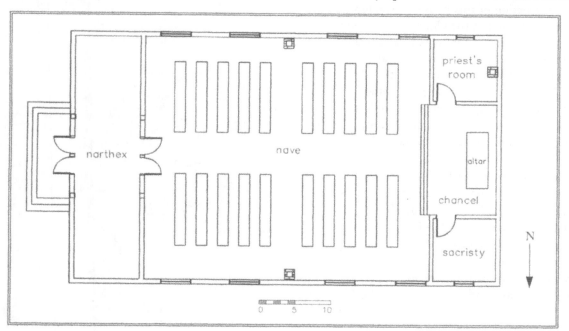

miles away. Although such transport was not an unusual necessity in frontier construction, this project required a great many trips to the building site by wagons loaded with 18-foot-by-2-inch-by-6-inch boards for joists and rafters, heavy timbers for posts, and 1-inch boards for sheathing and flooring, thereby prolonging the schedule. Relying on their knowledge of recent developments in frame construction with milled lumber and nails as well as on their experience and skill in building large-scale barns, the local carpenters fashioned a heavy wooden frame of 2-by-6-inch studs set 24 inches on center. To secure the frame in place and to satisfy conservative building practices, the workers probably mortised the studs into a heavy sill and braced them firmly at the corners of the building as well as between each stud. The bell-tower section of the church involved heavier timbers, of 6 by 6 inches or 8 by 8 inches, mortised together and integrated into the external frame and the narthex wall not only to support the weight of the tower and spire but also to secure the 1,068-pound bell that was hoisted in place when the framework was complete.[18]

Figure 2:8
Sawmill, south of Meire Grove, ca. 1875

The construction of this house of worship, which was dedicated as the Church of St. John the Baptist, indicated a coming-of-age for the community both in terms of its material growth and its abiding dedication to the Catholic faith. The simplicity of the edifice's exterior and its broad, squat elevation reflect a grass-roots vernacular aesthetic not directly influenced by sophisticated taste. Basically, the church resembled a barn to which Gothic arched windows, portal, bell tower, and spire were attached. But whatever its formal or stylistic qualities, the real achievement of the building lay in the fact that local craftsmen, who had not previously worked on a project of this scale, were able to define and solve the construction problems it presented.

As milled lumber and mass-produced cut nails became locally available, it became feasible

Figure 2:9a
Henry and Mary Imdieke farmhouse, Getty Township, as remodeled for use as a granary

to build houses and other types of structures using balloon-frame construction. Early in the 1870s, a sawmill operating south of Meire Grove began providing limited amounts of lumber for the local market (fig. 2:8). After the St. Paul, Minneapolis and Manitoba Railroad came through nearby Melrose in 1871, one could readily secure pine boards, cut nails, and other materials for frame construction from the Borgerding Lumber Yard there. Despite the several-year-long economic depression that began in 1873 and the locust plagues that ended in 1877, some farm families in the parish were able to acquire the necessary materials to replace their log dwellings with frame houses or to build additions to their cabins.

Henry and Mary Imdieke lived with their five children in a one-story frame house, dating to about 1872–75, that measured just 26

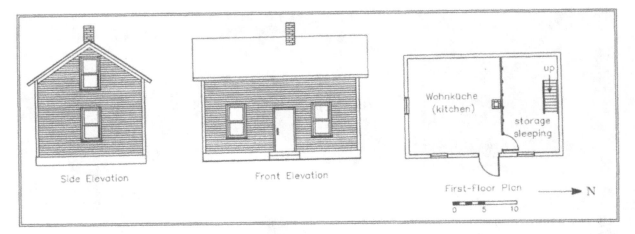

by 16 feet (figs. 2:9a, 2:9b).[19] Three oak logs laid horizontally on the ground acted as a foundation, on which a 4-by-6-inch sill supported full-dimension 2-by-8-inch joists and 2-by-4-inch studs set 16 inches on center. Cut-iron nails joined the pieces of the frame. The main interior walls were finished with lath and plaster; a thin wall made of 1-by-6-inch boards divided the space into two rooms. Opening the dwelling's only door, one entered directly into an all-purpose kitchen area near whose center were a chimney and a cooking/heating range. Behind this room was a sleeping-and-storage area containing a staircase that ascended to a loft; the roof rafters and boards comprised an unfinished ceiling. Windows on the east and west ends of the house brought in light and air on both levels. This simple dwelling resembles a hut or shelter for a hired man. Indeed, in the northwestern German provinces the same type of structure was called *ein Heuerhaus,* a small house inhabited by a peasant who lived on and worked the land for the master of the farm. Although the Imdiekes' 160-acre tract promised ample economic means, they seem to have elected a household economy so severe as to allow only for absolute essentials.

August and Anna Illies, one of the parish's founding couples, constructed a simple one-and-a-half story balloon-frame house in 1876 (fig. 2:10). The structure was typical of the first moderately scaled dwellings that settlers in the region could afford. The Illieses divided

Figure 2:9b
First-floor plan and elevations, Henry and Mary Imdieke farmhouse, Getty Township, built ca. 1872–75

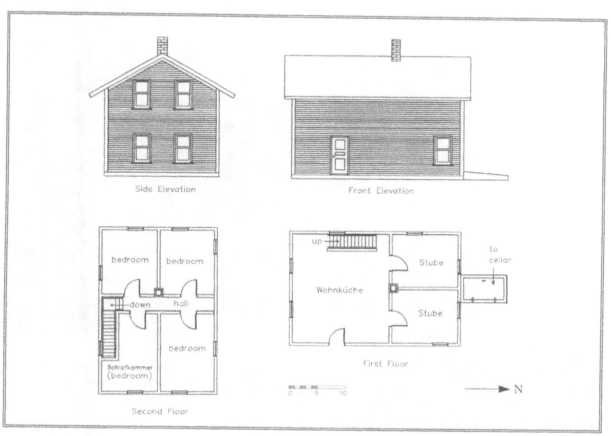

Side Elevation

Front Elevation

bedroom   bedroom

down   hall

bedroom

Schlafkammer
(bedroom)

Second Floor

up

Stube

to
cellar

Wohnküche

Stube

First Floor

0   5   10

→ N

Figure 2:10
Floor plan and elevations, August and
Anna Illies farmhouse, Grove Township,
built 1876

the 22-by-31-foot enclosure into two kinds of spaces—one large *Wohnküche,* centering on the *Herdfeuer,* and six chambers used for storage and as bedrooms (*Stuben* and *Schlafkammern*). This "no-frills" plan adequately accommodated the couple and their six children. The division of first-floor space was similar to that in the Imdieke house and virtually identical to that in the Zenzen log cabin. Like Zenzen, the builders of the Illies house remembered the spatial template of the *Pfostenwohnhaus* model and adapted it to the frame-construction technique; likewise, they used the "modern" iron cooking/heating range available in America to perform the role of the customary central hearth. According to the 1870 U.S. Census,

Figure 2:11
Henry Gramke house, Meire Grove;
addition under construction, ca. 1900

two German-American carpenters were then working in Grove Township. It may have been one of these craftsmen who creatively adapted the "old ways" to the new conditions. If not, the Illieses, like most German-American farmers, were able planners and builders and could well have designed and built the house. August and Anna may have planned the re-creation of an interior that was easily remembered from their German villages, still familiar and domestically comfortable. The early Zenzen, Imdieke, and Illies houses established a link between past and present, perpetuating a traditional interior framed in frontier and modern systems of building.[20]

A photograph from about 1900 showing carpenters working on an addition to the Henry Gramke house in Meire Grove documents how suitable balloon-frame construction was for the growing community (fig. 2:11). The Henry Meyer farmhouse, located just south of the village, was another balloon-frame structure of the kind commonly built in the parish during the 1870s and 1880s (fig. 2:12). The wings of these houses, added as families grew,

Figure 2:12
Henry Meyer farmhouse, Grove Township,
built and added to ca. 1870–1900

formed either an L or a T configuration, with an elevation of one-and-a-half stories. In the 1870s the Meyer farmhouse was similar to the Imdieke house described above. The small dwelling had only a downstairs kitchen and bedrooms on the half-story; that unit is shown here on the left. The center section, added in the 1880s, provided a dining room and more bedrooms. When Henry retired, his son and family, who now worked the farm and lived in the house, built a small wing on the right that he occupied during his last years.

When parish farmers built balloon-frame houses in the 1890s and early 1900s, they tailored popular models to meet local needs and preferences. Carpenters living in the parish constructed the Joseph Ellering farmhouse in about 1900 following a design similar to those found in popular house catalogs published by Sears, Roebuck and Company and Montgomery Ward, or a plan book issued by a nearby lumberyard (fig. 2:13). The broad structure is a basic two-story T-plan, elaborated with dormers, a bay window,

and a Doric-columned porch. The Fred Butler farmhouse in Getty
Township exemplifies another type popular in the 1890s and early
1900s (fig. 2:14). It is a Foursquare design, so named for its simple
two-story cubical shape and pyramidal roof. The floor plan also
reflects a foursquare symmetry and balance. This design promised
efficiency and comfort at a low cost. A distinctively local feature of
the Butler farmhouse is its stucco exterior surface. This finish no
doubt satisfied the family's desire to give the house an appearance
of strength and stability that the white-clapboard siding of most
balloon-frame structures failed to generate.

Between 1870 and 1880, the size of the parish "family" doubled to
include approximately one hundred families, or about one thousand
people. After paying an outstanding debt on the frame church, a
newly appointed parish priest, Father Meinulf Stuckenkemper
began raising funds to erect a second Church of St. John the
Baptist. In a previous post in the Diocese of St. Cloud the priest

Figure 2:14
Fred Butler farmhouse, Getty Township,
built ca. 1910

had successfully carried out a project to build St. Mary's Church in St. Cloud, recognized at the time as one of the largest and most beautiful Catholic sanctuaries in Minnesota. Working with a building fund of $5,000 and a $100-per-family pledge, he directed parishioners in the construction of the new church. Contracts were let in the winter of 1885. Soon afterward, excavation of the basement began as parishioners hauled granite stones from surrounding farmland for the foundation. Farmers' and merchants' wagons also carried lumber, brick and mortar, and lath and plaster from Melrose to the building site at the intersection of Oak Grove and Church Streets. The Imdieke brickworks, operating on a farm north of town since about 1881, supplied brick for the project.

The church plan designated a neo-Gothic structure, 62 feet wide and 120 feet long, with a steeple that rose to a height of 156 feet— an elevation that enabled virtually everyone in the parish to see the church from their farms (figs. 2:15a, 2:15b).[21] The planning and

supervision of a project of this scale and
complexity was clearly beyond the
resources of local craftsmen.[22] Father
Meinulf commissioned a St. Cloud architect, A. E. Hussey, to draw up plans and
specifications.[23] Hussey had had a firm in
Stearns County since the 1870s and was
characterized as "a scientific architect" who
"has for many years been a practical
builder, [and] is in every way competent to
plan and superintend the erection of all
kinds of buildings having always in view,
economy, strength, and beauty."[24]

John Kropp, a contractor and brickmason from St. Cloud, became the supervisor
of a crew of local bricklayers who laid up
the materials to veneer the heavy timber-
frame walls of the sanctuary.[25] The carpenter, Carl Lethert, directed construction of
that frame and the complex ceilings of the
nave and side aisles. Following his special-
ty, Lethert also constructed the complicated frame of the steeple.[26]

One might think that a building project
of this scale would have brought a wide
range of people into the parish as laborers
and thus exposed parishioners to the world
beyond its borders. However, except for the
architect, everyone who worked on the

Figure 2:15a
Church of St. John the Baptist,
Meire Grove, built 1885

church was German-American and Catholic. The quality of
builders' ethnic *Kameradschaftlichkeit* (comradeship) is evident in a
photograph of laborers and bricklayers working on a project in
Meire Grove that was taken a few years after the church was built
(fig. 2:16). Surrounded by his crew, the head craftsman or mason
toasts the beginning of the job with a glass of dark brew. Such rituals could have been performed at sacred as well as secular projects.
Skilled workmen such as these supplied the practical experience, the

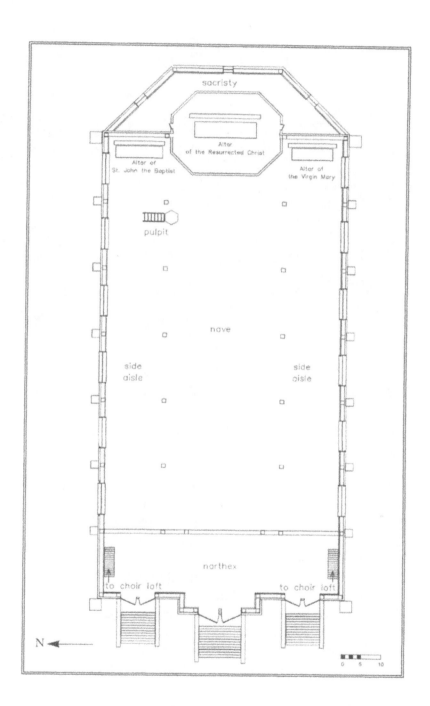

sacristy

Altar
of the Resurrected Christ

Altar of
St. John the Baptist

Altar of
the Virgin Mary

pulpit

nave

side
aisle

side
aisle

narthex

to choir loft

to choir loft

N

0   5   10

Figure 2:15b
Reconstruction of floor plan, Church of
St. John the Baptist, built 1885

Figure 2:16
Bricklayers at work, Meire Grove, ca. 1890

know-how, to transform Hussey's two-dimensional plan and elevation into a tangible architectural space. Although they worked for a daily wage, they also earned satisfaction through their awareness of the qualitative change their labors afforded the entire community.

From 1885 to 1900, the congregation continued donating funds for the appointment of the interior of the church, commissioning skilled workmen to stencil gilded decoration on the walls and ceiling, and hiring cabinetmakers and wood-carvers to make two elaborate side altars for the east end of the sanctuary (fig. 2:17). Two large confessional booths, finished with Gothic decoration, flanked each other in the side aisles. Family subscriptions paid for thirty-six hand-carved Bavarian statues that were set in niches around the inner perimeter. Further offerings provided for the installation of stained-glass windows. The sounds of a new 1,186-pipe organ enriched the liturgy of the Mass. Two bells in the church tower called the faithful to worship on Sunday and marked the celebration of the Mass on weekdays.[27] Their ringing also could be heard across the countryside on special feast days, such as Corpus Christi or Rogation Days, when parishioners gathered to celebrate the power of the saints who, they believed, protected and provided for them as they labored on their farms.[28]

When Father Meinulf selected the architect for the church, he also chose the architectural style in which it would be built. The second Church of St. John the Baptist was similar to others in the Diocese of St. Cloud and reflected the Gothic revival style that was popular in America during the second half of the nineteenth century.[29] It also bore a likeness to such *Hallenkirchen* (Gothic parish churches) in the northwestern German provinces as Sts. Peter and

Figure 2:17
Interior, Church of St. John the Baptist, Meire Grove, ca. 1900

Paul in Holdorf, built in 1858 (fig. 2:18). Both structures have a central bell tower marking the main entrance to the sanctuary as well as buttressing on the brick walls between the pointed arch windows. The furnishing of the Meire Grove church interior, on the other hand, directly expressed parishioners' tastes for elaborate combinations of plasterwork, wood-carving, stencil decoration, painting, and colored windows. Illumination from those windows and from the golden light of candles in the chandeliers hanging from the ceiling of the nave created an environment qualitatively different from any that the parishioners experienced in their everyday lives. The result was similar to a Gothic splendor that many had experienced in Catholic cathedrals and parish churches in their native provinces.[30]

Parishioners believed that the sanctuary of the Church of St. John the Baptist was the one place where a person could experience order and regularity. Despite the abundance of objects, furnishings, and ornament in the church, congregants perceived that everything there had its proper place and its appropriate time in the celebration of the Mass. The three altars containing carved figures presented worshipers with an organized series of biblical images that stimulated a proper piety. On the central altar, at the highest register, stood a figure of the risen Christ. Immediately below him to the right and left were St. John the Baptist and St. John the Evangelist, respectively. The level of the altar nearest the celebrants of the Mass contained figures of the Virgin Mary and Mary Magdalene, accompanied by a pair of angels pointing heavenward to the resurrected Christ. St. John the Baptist was venerated on the side altar on the left. As patron saint, John, who had sojourned in the wilderness, would understand the prayers of those who struggled as pioneers in a new land. The side

Figure 2:18
Church of Sts. Peter and Paul, Holdorf,
Oldenburg, Germany, built 1858

altar on the right was dedicated to the congregation's other major intercessor and protector, Mary, the Mother of Christ. Parishioners watched as the priest, standing to the right of the central altar near the Virgin's side altar, read the Gospel at its given point in the service each Sunday; he delivered the Epistle standing on the left, near the side altar of St. John the Baptist. The Stations of the Cross depicting the Passion of Christ, set on the sanctuary walls in an order ordained by Church tradition and authority, directed one's steps and patterned one's devotions. Virtually every element in the worship service and in the house of worship was fixed within a seemingly eternal order that generated a sense of security in the worshiper. The structure itself, however, was not everlasting. During a blizzard on the night of Tuesday, February 13, 1923, the building and all it contained was destroyed by fire.[31]

A comparison of the two previous churches with the one built in 1885 reflects the steady growth of the parish. The log church enclosed 540 square feet and held about thirty worshipers. The third, elaborately appointed structure enclosed almost seventy-five hundred square feet and could accommodate fifteen hundred worshipers.[32] Such a comparison can only suggest the vivid sense of energy that parishioners felt as they watched their churches become increasingly large and, finally, quite splendid. For those who had helped establish the community and make it secure, the increase may have seemed like the fulfilling of a covenant with God: Having honored Him with a fine house, parishioners could feel more secure in believing that He also had some obligations toward His chosen people.

As noted above in relation to the building of the church, an important local industry originated in the early 1880s when Herman and Joseph Imdieke collaborated in a venture to produce bricks for farm and business buildings. Both Herman and Joseph had worked at brickyards in Cincinnati before arriving in Minnesota, in 1869 and 1870, respectively. According to his grandson, Herman thought of starting a brickyard while using clay and straw to chink the openings in the walls of his log house. The mental image of a substantial brick home on his farm may have been his incentive to begin experimenting with local materials to achieve a proper recipe

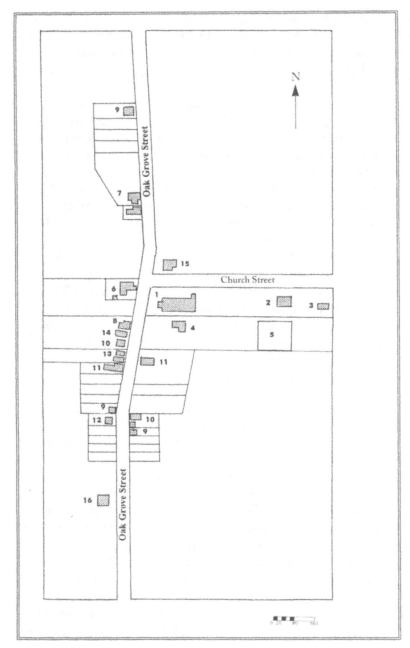

Figure 2:19
Meire Grove, 1900
1. Church of St. John the Baptist, built 1885
2. Site of 1871 Church of St. John the Baptist
3. Site of 1864 log church
4. Priest's house
5. Cemetery
6. Schoolhouse
7. Hotel and stables
8. Blacksmith shop
9. Residence
10. Saloon
11. General store
12. Meire Grove Cooperative Dairy Association
13. Shoe shop
14. Harness shop
15. Henry Imdieke farm
16. Henry Meyer farm

Figure 2:20
Oak Grove Street, Meire Grove, ca. 1900;
Clemens Meyer's general store in foreground

for quality brick.[33] That search for a good product involved the brothers, with varied results, from about 1881 to 1885.[34]

The construction of the third parish church prompted the Imdiekes to pursue their trade until they achieved satisfactory results. Father Meinulf contracted with them to supply brick for the structure's inner walls.[35] The project launched a business that would contribute significantly both to the material well-being and the physical appearance of the rural parish. From 1881 until 1915, when it stopped production, the Imdieke brickyard supplied materials for stores and shops in the village and for thirty-six houses on surrounding farms.

By 1896, the year Meire Grove became an incorporated village, it bore a look of stability and permanence. Places of business along Oak Grove Street, the one and only thoroughfare, were built of Imdieke brick (fig. 2:19). A photograph of the street from about 1900 shows stores and shops located on lots that had been platted by the first village council (fig. 2:20). A wooden sidewalk on the

Figure 2:21
Holdorf, Oldenburg, Germany, 1990

west side of the street and some hitching posts border the unpaved avenue, which, in less traversed places, nurtures patches of grass. Horse-drawn wagons await their owners, who are presumably busy at a general store or relaxing in a saloon. By 1900, following village incorporation, the sidewalk also guided parishioners to a post office and some, on occasion, to a jail. General-merchandise stores, blacksmith shops, a harness shop, wagon shop, shoe shop, two saloons, and the Meire Grove Cooperative Dairy Association served the essential needs of rural life. A few houses and two farmsteads operating within the village limits were also on the main street.[36] The yellow glow of a few gaslights illuminated the thoroughfare after dark. The large Gothic church marked the center of the community. A rectory just south of the church housed the clergy. The earth just east of church and rectory was sanctified as the parish cemetery. The village was not entirely self-sufficient but was adequate for residents' physical and spiritual requirements.

The scale, shape, and design of Meire Grove and the farmlands surrounding it parallel the dispersed layout of farms and villages in northwestern Germany. Comparing the views and plans of Meire Grove and those of Holdorf, the village in Oldenburg from which many local residents originated, reveals various similarities. Holdorf's spired church, like the one in Meire Grove, is situated at a central

Figure 2:22
Holdorf, Oldenburg, 1858
1. *Church of Sts. Peter and Paul*
2. *Priest's house*
3. *Gasthaus (tavern)*
4. *Stables*
5. *Residence*
6. *Bricklayer's house*
7. *Carpenter's house*
8. *Hallenhaus (farm)*
9. *Blacksmith's house*

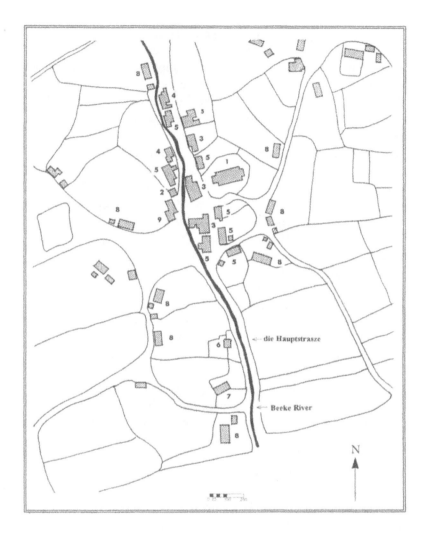

intersection or square. In the German village, too, places of business and farms are located on both sides of the main road (figs. 2:21, 2:22).[37] This comparison is not meant to imply that the immigrants who pioneered in Stearns County settled in an area that resembled their homeland. In 1858, before Meire Grove existed, there would have been little in the condition and appearance of the land to remind them of the way things looked in the northwestern German provinces. While there were open lands, stands of trees, and underbrush in the provinces, these were present as a result of centuries of cultivation. Similarities between the two places now exist because Meire Grove villagers and farmers actively formed their environment according to principles of order learned in the Old World.[38]

The 1896 plats of the area indicate the location and size of farms that averaged one hundred sixty acres, with some landholdings as small as eighty and others as large as two hundred forty acres (fig. 2:23). Homesteaders tended to settle on forty-acre parcels that overlapped sections and quarter-sections, creating zigzag boundaries along property lines. When looking for a homestead, the German pioneer does not seem to have been sympathetic to the logic of the survey and geometric plat of the land. Rather, sites appear to have been selected according to their potential for success: acreage containing some tillable land, open meadows, stands of trees for building and fuel, and prospects for good water. Farms developed on sites near but separate from villages. Despite the order of the grid system that defines tracts of land in the parish, the locations of farmsteads seem to be somewhat random (fig. 2:24). Because township roads curve and change elevation as they follow or traverse the gently rolling northwest-southeast undulations of the land, farmsteads can be seen from a variety of perspectives. As one travels through the countryside, views of farmsteads offer prospects in which picturesque asymmetries and irregularities conceal the rigid geometry of platted sections of land.

Within a period of two generations, from 1858 to 1915, the German-Americans of St. John the Baptist parish moved from subsistence agriculture to successful dairy farming. Initially, they sheltered themselves in primitive dugout dwellings or simple log cabins. Later, they built balloon-frame houses and, in many cases,

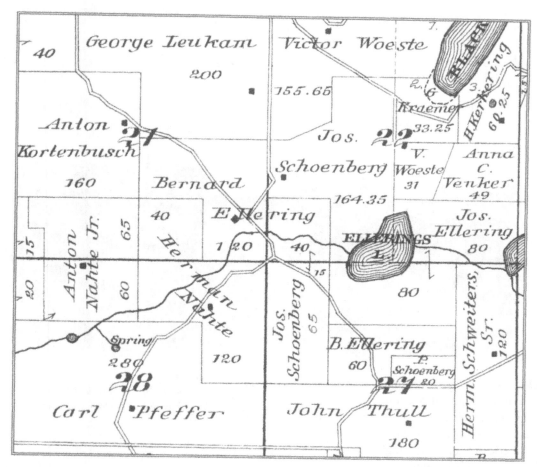

Figure 2:23
Plat of Grove Township, 1896 (detail)

ultimately constructed substantial brick homes. The village, though small, was sufficient to meet their immediate practical needs. Their place of worship, so important in a Catholic parish, went through successive stages of development, culminating in the large, lavishly appointed brick sanctuary that accommodated every member of the congregation.

A summary of the stages of growth, kinds of buildings, and methods of construction in the parish suggests that the community is part of an all-American rural landscape. The farms and the village

appear as such, unless one discerns important interior features of the structures that reveal a vital continuation of traditional German ways of building. These are manifested in the creation and use of space as well as in construction methods and materials. Both German and American traits of the built landscape are important in the parish. A synthesis of elements of both cultures created a remarkable environment in which new approaches to building were employed while the essential qualities of traditional folk architecture were preserved.

Figure 2:24
Norman Wehlage and Daniel Meyer farms,
Getty Township (view from southwest),
1990

111

III. MAKING BRICK
AND BUILDING HOUSES

Sixteenth-Century Brick
Manufacture, *woodcut, n.d.*

Until the early 1880s, when the Imdieke brothers began manufacturing brick on Herman's farm, families in St. John the Baptist parish could choose to build houses using materials and construction processes that were familiar to them from their native villages and towns in the northwestern German provinces and from German-American settlements where they had stayed on their way to Minnesota. Herman and Joseph came to Meire Grove from Holdorf in Oldenburg by way of Cincinnati. When they arrived in Stearns County, in 1869 and 1870, respectively, each had sufficient funds to purchase farmland north of the village. The parish celebrated a double wedding for the brothers and their brides in 1873. The Imdieke name was becoming established in the community.

Joseph learned the brickmaking trade in the northwestern German provinces. Both brothers worked in a brickyard in Cincinnati during their four years in that city's German community.[1] Their initial effort at pursuing the craft in the parish resulted in failure. During the first firing, in 1880 or 1881, bricks exploded because they contained lime. Apparently the brothers had used a clay that was dug from a depth where the material contained too much stone sediment.[2]

Accounts depicting the brothers abandoning the brickyard for several years after that failed first firing seem implausible.[3] Given their previous experience, they probably anticipated a period in which they would have to experiment and adjust their knowledge of the trade to local materials and conditions. They likely knew that they would have to learn to quarry and temper a purer clay and mix it with the proper proportion of sand if they wanted to obtain satisfactory results. Also, the firing of the kiln had to be controlled at the right temperatures for the proper amounts of time. Once they achieved this level of expertise, they would be better able to recognize and sort out inferior bricks and thus provide a quality building product to the community.

Herman and Joseph pursued their experimentation during 1881 and 1882. Batches of brick made during this time showed variable quality but also indicated consistent improvement. Henry, the youngest of the Meire Grove Imdiekes, may have not had any direct involvement in the brickyard, but his farmhouse, built in the village in 1883, was the first structure there made of Imdieke brick. Three different grades of material are evident in the house, which still stands: soft brick in the north and east walls; hard brittle brick in the south and west walls; and quality brick in the kitchen and summer kitchen east wing (fig. 4:11a).[4]

Sometime in 1884 or 1885, Herman hired Ignatz Greve, an experienced brickmaker, who helped formulate the best recipe using local materials and probably advised on how to build and fire a brick kiln. In 1885 Father Meinulf Stuckenkemper, the parish priest, commissioned an architect and hired a stonemason and carpenter to plan and supervise the construction of the second Church of St. John the Baptist. He also contracted to buy brick for the project from the Imdiekes.

As the general demand for brick increased following construction of the church, Herman hired between ten and fifteen workers for the various tasks of quarrying, mixing, molding, and firing the brick. He made agreements with farmers in the parish to trade a winter month's labor of cutting and hauling kiln firewood for a portion of the bricks needed to build their houses.[5] In 1898 he purchased a machine from Cincinnati that molded raw clay into individual bricks, enabling him to increase production to between fifteen and twenty thousand bricks per day. A twenty-horsepower engine ran the machine; a fifteen-horsepower engine mounted on a wagon cut wood needed for the increased number of firings at the factory.[6] The new machine eased the labor and shortened the annual manufacturing period. The quantity produced each year seems to have remained fairly constant.

During the three decades that the brick factory stayed open, Herman and his wife, Agnes, also ran their 120-acre farm. Some of the men who labored in the brickyard also worked as hired hands on the farm. From about 1910 to 1915, Herman's seven sons took on jobs in the brickyard. By that time, like most other parish farmers, Herman had developed a herd of dairy cows. He and his family met the steady demands of that kind of farming in addition to the seasonal labors of the brickyard. Herman ran the yard for about two and a half months during spring and summer, or according to demand—except when the weather was too cold to permit kiln-firing. Starting in 1885, he charged $5 per 1,000 bricks, raising the price to $6 in 1915, the year he closed the operation.[7] By then, his sons had left the homeplace and were situated on farms elsewhere in the parish or county. Further, wages for labor had multiplied while demand for bricks declined.

Varying accounts of the origins of this local enterprise suggest the fallibility of human memory. Inaccuracies of recall would not be unusual given the complexity of the process, which necessitated some trial-and-error before good brick could be produced.[8] Brickmaking began during the fall with the hard labor of digging

Figure 3:1
Herman and Joseph Imdieke brick factory,
Grove Township, ca. 1890

Figure 3:1a
Imdieke brick factory pug mill (center) and offbearer with molder forms (right). Part of the shed roof over the kiln is visible behind the two horses.

Figure 3:1b
Two of Herman Imdieke's sons (left foreground). The drying sheds and racks are visible behind the men and horses.

clay from a pit or quarry and hauling the heavy material by horse-drawn wagon to an open area near the brickyard, where it was spread out to weather for a period of months. Laborers periodically cut the heaps of clay into sections and turned them over so that the raw material was thoroughly exposed to the elements. Rain and frost disintegrated and softened it as well as washed out any excess salts or flux.[9] Once the clay was properly cured, it was hauled to the brickyard. A photograph dating from about 1890 shows Herman (on the far left) and two of his young sons standing in the brickyard as a wagon (on the right, behind the boys) brings in a load of tempered clay (fig. 3:1). When workers shoveled the raw material into the pug mill, a machine used for mixing the basic ingredients, the brickmaker added proper amounts of water and sand for a thorough blend of the thick material that resulted from the circular motion of the wheel and mixing blades that the team of horses pulled around and around.

A detail of the photograph shows two Imdieke employees standing on either side of the pug mill (fig. 3:1a). They hold the wooden forms, whose divisions the molder first either moistened with water or sprinkled with sand (to facilitate removal of the raw brick) and then packed with soft mud clay from the mill. Each mold was about 20 percent larger than the size of the finished brick; this compensated for the shrinkage that occurred during drying and firing. Next, an offbearer scraped excess clay from the mold and carried the unit to the sheds immediately behind the yard (fig. 3:1b; the structures behind the men and horses). There he removed and stacked the brick on racks to dry. Drying brick under a shelter rather than in direct sunlight helped increase its strength. The brickmaker constructed a kiln from raw bricks under a protective shed roof, which is visible in figure 3:1a behind the two horses that power the pug mill.

Construction of a clamp kiln (also known as a scove kiln, fig. 3:2) prepared for the burning, or firing, of the dried brick at the Imdieke factory. Brickmakers stacked between thirty-five and forty thousand raw bricks in patterns that formed arches or fireboxes at the base of the structure (fig. 3:3). The dimensions of a fully constructed kiln ranged from 30 to 50 feet long, from 20 to 35 feet wide, and from 12

Figure 3:2
Scove kiln, Kugel brick factory, St. Cloud,
ca. 1868

Figure 3:3
Scove kiln firebox construction

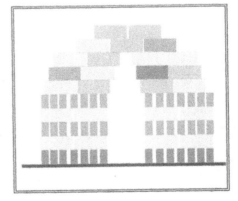

to 18 feet high.[10] The kilns built at the Imdieke factory were modeled after an updraft type then in general use throughout Northern Europe. The patterning of bricks inside the kiln provided air spaces through which the heat and gases could pass during firing. The basic principles of stacking brick in the kiln were to ensure the best draft and fuel combustion, prevent fire marks from darkening the bricks, and achieve the best and most even heat distribution.[11] Around the outer perimeter of the pile, the brickmaker set the raw bricks close together, and he sometimes coated the exterior of the pile with mud to seal the sides of the kiln. The top of the kiln was not sealed; this was so that the convection from the fireboxes spread throughout the interior of the structure. In addition to keeping heat in the kiln, the mud covering prevented drafts from intensifying temperatures in certain areas of the kiln and affecting the quality of the finished brick.

Firing began when workers ignited the wood in the fireboxes at the base of the kiln. The brickmaker brought the temperature up slowly to vaporize any moisture remaining in the raw brick; clouds of steam rose from the top of the kiln. When the steam emission stopped, the fires were fed until the temperature climbed to between 1,400 and 1,800 degrees Fahrenheit. At this stage, two things happened: The heat consumed any combustible material in the brick; and the characteristic red-orange color that distinguished Imdieke brick appeared, as ferrous oxides in the clay turned into ferric oxide. A firing range that pushed temperatures in the kiln to more than 2,000 degrees Fahrenheit vitrified the clay, and the bricks shrank further. When the brickmaker decided that the kiln had settled enough during this final shrinkage, he extinguished the fires and let the kiln cool for three or more days. At this point, he could also cover the top of the kiln with mud to seal in and hold the heat evenly in every part of the kiln during the cooling period.

Once cooled, the bricks were sorted. Some at the bottom of the pile cracked or were crushed by the weight of the kiln. Bricks on the outer edges were too soft, while those near the center emerged too hard and brittle.[12] A quality brick is hard and well burned, regular in shape with sharp edges and corners, gives a clear ring when struck, is free of lime and lumps of impurities, and is virtually nonabsorbent.[13] An Imdieke brick measured 7½ by 2⅛ by 3½ inches.[14]

No two firings were exactly alike, resulting in bricks that were unique to a particular kiln. Fuel consumption for a burning at the Imdieke kiln of fifty thousand bricks could consume fifteen or sixteen cords of hardwood (a supply measuring 120 by 60 by 60 feet).[15] How a firing was adjusted as it proceeded and the percentage of quality brick it yielded were determined by the brickmaker's knowledge and experience.

The brickmaker tried to predict stable weather conditions for a firing. Strong, gusty winds would make it difficult to control fuel combustion. Heavy rain could deluge the exterior of the kiln, causing the kiln brick to crack and flake during baking and cooling.

People who lived in the village and on nearby farms experienced the sound, sight, and smells from the Imdieke brickyard during the days and nights when a firing was under way.[16] The kiln fires must have appeared especially bright in the darkness of the countryside. The soft yellow glow of kerosene lamps indoors or the gas tapers of the village street lamps were dim compared to the brilliance emanating from the brickyard north of the village. This tangible, visible evidence of the industry must have assured parishioners that the community was truly established and promised a secure future. The firm, hard, substantial nature of the product enabled them to build homes that would embody a permanency that paralleled their tenure on the land.

The controlled, regularized, repeated, seasonal process of making brick seemed to suit the temperament of these German-Americans. As one with much experience in the trade observed:

> *To be a successful brickmaker a man must have more than ordinary physical strength and energy; he must have a sound, deliberating judgement; he must have industry, persistency, patience, and endurance; he must be watchful, temperate, and discriminating; and above all, he must want to, and determine to master the art.*[17]

Clearly, brickmaking demanded an enormous labor to obtain a product of quality. The various levels of experience and skill, together with the patience and endurance of every worker, contributed to good results. The brickmaker had to have a conceptual and practical image of the entire kiln as he stacked tens of thousands of raw bricks to form the structure. He also had to understand the process that transformed the raw materials into *der Backstein* (baked stone). In creating the structure and controlling the process at every step, the brickmaker was something of an alchemist, performing subtle acts of transformation to turn clay mud into firm, geometrically regular brick. His alchemy made it possible for parishioners to effect a transformation of their own, adapting traditional Northern European vernacular house types to new American architectural forms as they constructed their substantial brick homes.

When farm families in St. John the Baptist parish wanted to create such homes, they could rely upon skilled bricklayers and carpenters who lived in the community. These craftsmen operated farms or businesses but were also hired to work as teams for the building of houses, barns, and other structures. There was never a building boom per se in the parish. Rather, brick farmhouses replaced log cabins and frame houses from year to year at a steady pace, with brick supplied by the Imdieke yard. The average output from the Imdieke operation was one hundred fifty to two hundred thousand bricks per year.[18] About that many bricks were required each year for the farmhouses built from 1883 to 1915.

Families and builders integrated a schedule for construction into the seasonal cycles of farming. Whenever possible during the months before construction began, the farmer hauled glacial-granite boulders from his fields to the building site to be used for the foundation. Boulders of various sizes were right at hand; they emerged in the plowed fields each spring after frost action forced them up to the surface. While rock-picking was a difficult annual chore, the labor became somewhat satisfying when it went toward the construction of the family home. After harvest, the farmer, using a team of horses harnessed to a scoop, excavated for the foundation. The general shape, size, plan, and orientation of the house on the site had already been worked out between the family and the construction crew.[19] In building the foundation, the stonemason used a heavy sledgehammer to split and face the stones so that they were relatively flat on both their interior and exterior surfaces. He then selected, placed, and mortared the stones to make the foundation wall.

However difficult it was to haul the stone and construct the foundation, the dense granite provided the best and most durable material for the basement walls. As the least porous of stones, granite does not transmit water from the ground to the brick.[20] A foundation wall rising two to three feet above ground level virtually assured that no moisture would seep into the house's brick walls. Such seepage would create an unwholesome dampness in the house and eventually deteriorate the brick.

The builders did not work from blueprints or floor plans. It was said that planning and building a brick house "came to them as easy as eating."[21] The statement implies that these men had an appetite for building that was satisfied when a structure met the requirements of their craft and the needs and preferences of the farm family.

Planning and negotiations for a house were conducted in the native language. *Der Maurer* (bricklayer and wall-maker) and *der Zimmermann* (carpenter and room-maker) discussed with *der Bauer* (farmer) and *die Bauerin* (farm wife) the size and number of *die Schlafkammern* (bedrooms), *die Küche* (kitchen), and the need for *eine Eingangshalle* (entrance) or *ein Wohnzimmer* (living room). A thorough planning, guided by the experience of the bricklayer and carpenter, established the length and width of the house and its room dimensions so that sizes of lumber and amounts of brick could be specified, thereby limiting waste of labor and materials.[22] Horse-drawn wagons carried lumber from the local sawmill south of Meire Grove or from the Borgerding Lumber Yard in Melrose. Neighbors shared in the hauling effort, picking up building materials when returning from taking a load of grain to Melrose or doing errands in the village. Winter was a good time to haul the heavy loads of brick because the ground was frozen hard, and the horses did not overheat in the cold air. Four to five hundred bricks could be carried in a single load; as many as two hundred loads might be necessary to convey enough brick for a large dwelling, such as the Henry and Wilhelmina Haverkamp farmhouse in Getty Township (fig. 3:8a).[23]

Builders scheduled these stages of preparation so that the foundation could settle into place and the laying of brick could begin after spring planting. The bricklayer began construction by defining the outer perimeter of the walls with horizontal plumb lines. Using a vertical plumb line or a spirit level, he determined the mark at which to establish the corners of the house. He then laid up a few courses of brick at each of the four corners. Next, he set each course in the proper pattern until the wall reached the level of the first-story window sills.[24] Repeating the process with the vertical plumb line, the bricklayer increased the height of each corner and continued to follow a horizontal plumb line to lay the courses of brick in the intervening wall (fig. 3:4).[25]

One or more men mixed and carried the mortar and brick to the bricklayer as the structure rose from the foundation.[26] After the carpenters set the joists in the wall at the foundation level and covered them with rough flooring, they erected scaffolding on which the laborers and bricklayer worked. When the brick wall reached the appropriate level, carpenters set the joists for the second story and laid rough flooring. Laborers secured a strong ladder in the open stairwell for passage to the upper level. A simple gin made with lumber, pulley, and rope could also be used to hoist loads of brick to the second floor (fig. 3:5). Working together, the carpenters and bricklayer set and secured each joist into the wall by laying up brick around

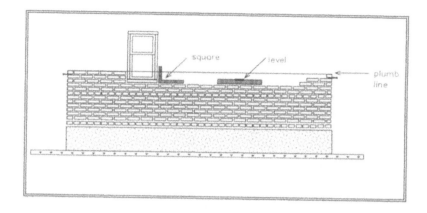

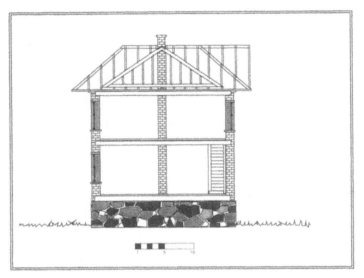

Figure 3:6
Cross section, John and Catherine
Schmiesing farmhouse under construction,
1904. See also figure 4:24a.

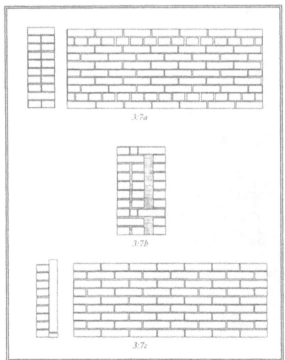

3:7a

3:7b

3:7c

Figure 3:7a
American common bond pattern

Figure 3:7b
Brick wall construction with air space

Figure 3:7c
Stretcher or running bond pattern

the 2-by-8-inch or 2-by-6-inch boards. The 7½-inch-long Imdieke bricks facilitated the 16-inches-on-center placement between each joist (i.e., two bricks plus mortar equaled 16 inches). When the walls reached their full elevation, the carpenters capped them with boards to which they nailed the roof rafters. They covered the rafters with boards and fastened on them shingles that had been split from local hardwoods. The interior walls of some houses were made of brick and surfaced with plaster, but most houses had interior frame walls covered with lath and plaster (fig. 3:6).

Local bricklayers used the American common bond pattern when making walls twelve to eighteen inches thick. Beginning with a course of headers (length of brick laid across the thickness of the wall) at the foundation level, the bricklayer set six courses of stretchers (length of brick laid lengthwise in the wall), then a seventh course of headers, repeating the pattern until the wall reached its designated height (fig. 3:7a). The headers at each seventh course tied together the two tiers of brick that composed the wall. Walls eighteen inches thick contained an insulating air space between the two outer courses and one inner course of brick. The bricklayer alternated header courses between inner and outer walls to tie the two together (fig. 3:7b). Frame structures could be veneered with a single layer of brick laid in a stretcher or running bond (fig. 3:7c).

The speed at which the brickmason laid courses of brick determined the pace of the entire project. Local builders probably did not try to establish and meet standards of efficiency but proceeded on the basis of doing the job in the right way. These craftsmen were, after all, working for and with their neighbors. They were not outsiders or entrepreneurs trying to minimize materials and wages in order to realize greater profits.[27]

Although parishioners seem to have primarily prized the skill of their bricklayers, the carpenters' abilities were equally important. They laid floors, built staircases, formed window frames, framed doorways and hung doors, and built cupboards and installed their shelves. Perhaps people took these features of the house for granted and placed greater value on the sound, substantial impression given by the patterning and thickness of the brick exterior walls.[28]

Figure 3:8a
Henry and Wilhelmina Haverkamp farm-
house, Getty Township, built 1899. See also
figure 5:6c.

Figure 3:8b
Floor plan, Haverkamp farmhouse

Most farm families in the Upper Midwest built balloon-frame houses. This simple, adaptable construction method, which took advantage of the abundance and affordability of lumber, readily met their needs and preferences.[29] About two-thirds of the farm families in St. John the Baptist parish constructed balloon-frame houses; others preferred and were able to build in brick. That option was open because of the locally available low-cost product made by the Imdieke factory.[30] At $5 per thousand, bricks for a house using about one hundred thousand of them would cost only $500. The cooperation of neighbors in hauling brick eliminated freight charges. Lumber, whether purchased from the local sawmill or the yard in Melrose, was also economical. The Haverkamp house is reported to have cost about $2,000 in 1899 (figs. 3:8a, 3:8b).[31] However, even considering the large size of the structure, this figure appears somewhat high. With approximately $500 spent on brick, about $700 for lumber, and wages for the stonemason, bricklayer, crew, carpenters, and laborers together totaling $500, the house probably cost about $1,700.[32] During a period when construction costs were stabilized, the price of a farmhouse of comparable size and complexity built of a wooden balloon frame would have been about $2,800 (figs. 3:9a, 3:9b).[33] Local claims that, in the early 1900s, it was cheaper to build a brick house than a frame house in the parish appear to be true.[34] The quantity of bricks that the Imdieke factory could produce in a year may have been the factor that limited the total number of brick farmhouses in the parish. The number built clearly indicates that demand steadily matched supply from the mid-1880s to 1915, when the factory closed.

As parish farm families planned their brick houses, they considered their various basic space needs. They required areas that would function for food storage and preparation and for the serving and eating of meals. Also included would be a parlor or living room to serve as a place for family devotions and for the religious shrines found in German Catholic homes as well as a place for social functions or meetings of church-related organizations. Many of the houses had three or more bedrooms, to accommodate large families. Bedrooms were also private places in which one could say the Rosary or novenas. Two laterally placed chimneys vented the cooking range

Figure 3:9a
Gundar and Elizabeth Lund farmhouse,
Lake Shore Township, Lac qui Parle
County, built ca. 1904

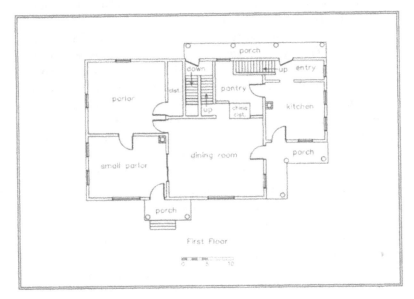

Figure 3:9b
First-floor plan, Lund farmhouse

in the kitchen and the heating stoves that were placed in the living room and second-story bedrooms. During the period when most of these houses were built, indoor plumbing was not a viable option. A hand pump and cistern supplied water for the kitchen sink and the portable metal tub, which was placed in the kitchen for baths. The outdoor privy served the other functions of a modern bathroom.

Brick farmhouses in St. John the Baptist parish were indigenous creations, the successful products of sustained hard labor and of processes that demanded experience and patience. Local craftsmen and laborers manufactured and processed construction materials at the local brickyard and sawmill, consulted in the design of the houses, and then helped build them. Construction was also facilitated, and made less costly, by the cooperative efforts of neighboring farmers who voluntarily hauled materials to the building site. The process of building up "big, beautiful brick houses," then, was a thoroughly communal effort. Through their creativity and cooperation, the German-Americans of the parish made houses that both preserved significant aspects of their vernacular building traditions and reflected a careful adaptation of useful aspects of selected American construction techniques.

IV

Herman and Agnes Imdieke
family and farmhouse,
Grove Township, ca. 1890

IV. DISTINCTIVE PARISH
FARM HOMES

The thirty-two houses in St. John the Baptist parish constructed of Imdieke brick were the most distinctive and characteristic features of the community's German-American Catholic culture (fig. 4:1).[1] Built from 1883 to 1915 during a period of stability and consolidation, these homes reflect the well-being of a community based on a sound agricultural economy. As significant architectural creations, they also embody the ethnic values, aesthetic preferences, and religious beliefs of the people who erected and lived in them.

This chapter and the two that follow it offer three perspectives on the meanings inherent in these structures as houses and as homes. In the present chapter, ten houses are documented through photographs and floor plans and are analyzed as representative of the whole. In four instances, descriptions of the relation of the given farmhouse to the barn and other outbuildings explain how the house functioned as a working unit of the farm. In Chapter Five a local vernacular aesthetic is inferred from qualities seen in individual houses, from features shared by members of the representative group, and from parishioners' aesthetic values as they themselves expressed them. In Chapter Six the sacred dimensions of the houses are interpreted within the context of a rural piety that recognized the dwellings' significance both as places where family members could perform devotions and as stages where parish priests could officiate at sacramentals. Understanding these structures as working units of a farm operation, as embodiments of a shared vision of beauty, and as places where the secular and sacred intersected will facilitate a full grasp of their meaning.

Identification of the parish's brick farmhouses according to type is an initial analytical task. A house type is determined by its basic

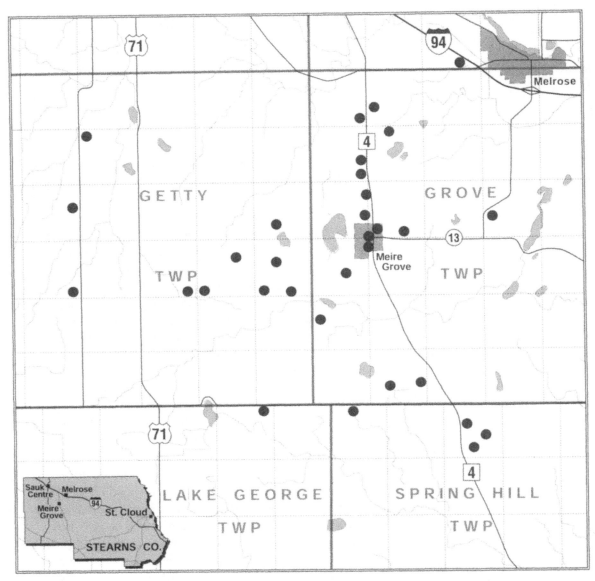

Figure 4:1
Locations of brick farmhouses built between 1883 and 1915 in Getty, Grove, Spring Hill, and Lake George Townships

structural shape or volume. With regard to these vernacular dwellings, this approach yields two general types: the cross-wing and the consolidated. Cross-wing houses are those in which one architectural mass extends from an equal or larger mass of the structure (figs. 3:8a, 4:3a, 4:4a, 4:6a, 4:11a). In the consolidated type, all interior spaces are contained within a single rectangular or square structural mass (figs. 4:19a, 4:20a, 4:22a, 4:24a, 4:25a). Each type will be further characterized here by extension and height, roof shape, and orientation of the given house on its site.

While being part of an American history of building, the brick farmhouses examined here exhibit a remarkable persistence of traditional forms and meanings in strong, simple architectural statements characteristic of a German-American vernacular heritage. Some of these dwellings may resemble traditional Anglo-American house types, while others appear to be fashionable picturesque designs derived from architectural stylebooks. But these similarities reflect only one aspect of the structures: their outward appearance. The German-American houses are essentially different from those types with respect to floor plans and use of interior space.[2]

A discussion of cross-wing dwellings in the parish will clearly illustrate their likenesses to a type popular in the Upper Midwest from the 1860s to the 1880s and will point up significant differences between national and local designs. Andrew Jackson Downing's *The Architecture of Country Houses* (1850), an American stylebook that offered plans and elevations for prospective builders, helped popularize the cross-wing house. Downing presented his picturesque design for "A Small Bracketed Cottage" in an appropriately sylvan landscape vignette (fig. 4:2). The right-angle projection of the wings in this house type afforded interesting profiles from a range of perspectives. A porch, bay window, bracketed eaves, and decorated chimneys were typical picturesque

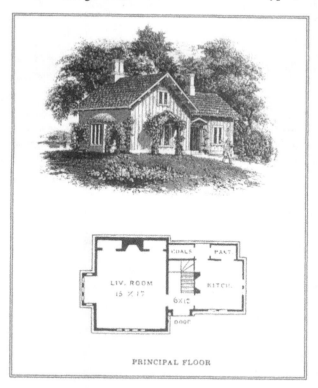

Figure 4:2
Andrew Jackson Downing, "A Small Bracketed Cottage," 1850

PRINCIPAL FLOOR

Figure 4:3a
August and Henry Illies farmhouse, Grove Township. This photograph was taken soon after a brick wing was added to the original frame structure in 1891. See also figure 2:10.

features that added a variety of texture and color and produced strong light-and-shadow contrasts on the exterior of the dwelling.

When the first and second generations of the Illies family expanded their farmhouse in Grove Township in 1891, it took on the appearance of Downing's design. This effect was mainly due to the building of an add-on wing, attached at right angles to the existing unit, to form a characteristic cross-wing configuration (fig. 4:3a).[3] August and Anna Illies had erected the original balloon-frame house in 1876; its traditional *Pfostenwohnhaus* floor plan and dual designation of rooms as kitchen and bedrooms are discussed in Chapter Two (fig. 2:10, first floor). The parents and six children were the first to occupy the *Schlafkammern* (bedrooms) and share the *Wohnküche* (all-purpose kitchen) of that dwelling; during the 1880s, the family grew to include nine children. August retired from farming in 1891 and turned the farm over to his eldest son, Henry. Because August and Anna intended to stay in their house, the family added a brick

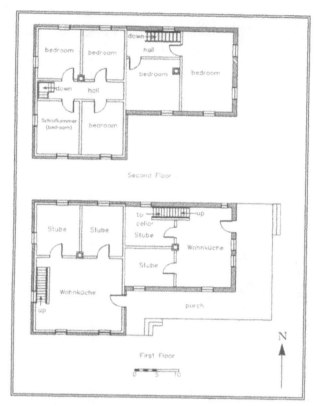

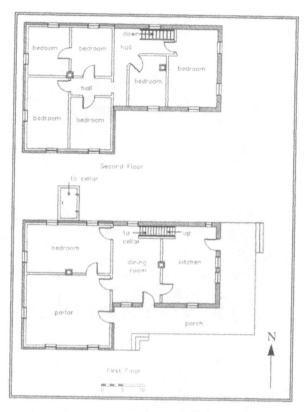

Figure 4:3b (left)
Floor plan, August and Henry Illies farmhouse, 1891

Figure 4:3c (right)
Floor plan, Henry Illies farmhouse, 1906

wing to the frame structure. The floor plan of this second unit duplicated the *Pfostenwohnhaus* design of the first one (fig. 4:3b). The house now had two kitchens and separate living quarters. With a veneer of brick applied to the original unit and with the embrace of a decorated wraparound porch, the remodeled structure looked like the kind of Victorian cottage Downing would have recommended. The core of the house at this and subsequent stages of development, however, remained distinctly German.

In 1906, when both August and Anna died, Henry and his wife, Mary, altered the interior to accommodate their family of eleven children.[4] Builders removed walls to enlarge rooms, eliminated the staircase in the original kitchen, and modified the access to the second-floor bedroom (fig. 4:3c). Despite this latter change, the basic

Figure 4:4a
Ferdinand Eveslage farmhouse, Spring Hill Township, built 1885–86

Figure 4:4b
Floor plan, Eveslage farmhouse

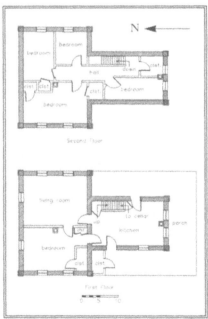

scheme on the first floor remained a simple division of space in which two rooms were focused on a central chimney. Doorways from the porch to the dining room and parlor were intended for guests. For just as in the first unit of the house, the actual front entrance was on the east wing, into the kitchen, directly relating kitchen work to the farmyard and barn chores.

The Ferdinand Eveslage farmhouse, built in Spring Hill Township in 1885–86, was another cross-wing brick dwelling extending symmetrically on its site in a T configuration. The two masses of the structure were defined by 15-inch-thick walls, realized in a single phase of construction (fig. 4:4a). The qualities of a balanced and proportioned plan were emphasized by the raised relief brick piers that accented each corner of the exterior walls. The main entrance was via the kitchen wing, which projected toward the farmyard court. The rear wing of the first floor had a living room and a bedroom (fig. 4:4b, bottom). Four bedrooms and closets upstairs were for the Eveslage children (fig. 4:4b, top).

Figure 4:5
Eveslage farmyard
1. *Farmhouse*
2. *Privy*
3. *Kitchen garden*
4. *Machine shed*
5. *Windmill and pump house*
6. *Chicken coop*
7. *Dairy barn*
8. *Heifer barn and feeding lot*

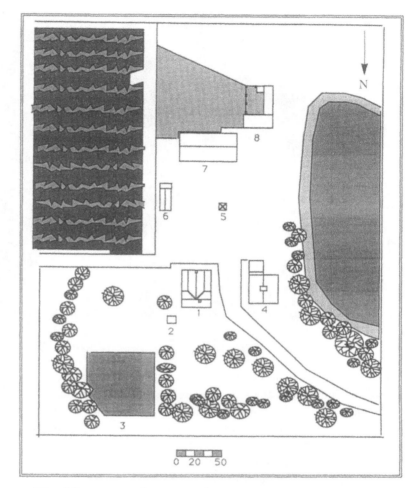

The fully appointed exterior of the house appeared similar to that of the Illies house (fig. 4:3a). A six-foot-wide frame porch, ornamented with millwork from the Borgerding Lumber Yard in Melrose, originally surrounded the kitchen wing. On such a picturesque porch, it was popularly assumed, one could relax and comfortably pursue cultured pastimes. But such aspects of the Victorian aesthetic do not seem to have suited the strenuously disciplined German-American Catholic farm family who built and inhabited the Eveslage house. The firm proportions of the design,

Figure 4:6a
Jacob and Elizabeth Botz farmhouse,
Getty Township, built 1888

the crisp contours defining strong volumes of brick walls, and the extended symmetry of the structure overall communicate a clear realization of form. Likewise, the barn and outbuildings south of the house were arranged so as to create an approximately symmetrical courtyard (fig. 4:5). Standing in the center of that open space today, one senses a physical as well as a spiritual equilibrium existing among all the structures on the site.

The Jacob and Elizabeth Botz farmhouse was in Getty Township, on the western edge of the parish. Its broad facade faced the country road but offered visitors no access from that approach (fig. 4:6a). As with most farmhouses in the parish, the front of the Botz dwelling was oriented toward the farmyard. One entered at the wing, either from the long porch on the east side or from the small west-side porch and doorway. Both portals introduced one into the heart of the house: the kitchen. Cooking aromas and the bustle of domestic work greeted family members and visitors as they walked in.

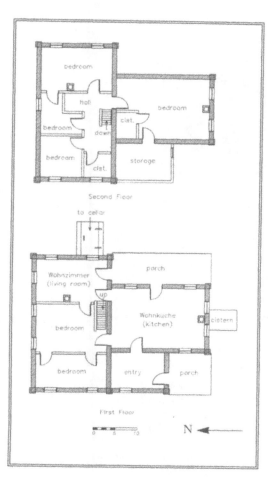

Figure 4:6b
Floor plan, Botz farmhouse

The first floor of the adjacent section of the Botz house contained a living room and two bedrooms (fig. 4:6b, bottom). One ascended to the second story, where there were four more bedrooms of varying size and some closet space (fig. 4:6b, top). The upper half of the doorway to the small bedroom on the west framed a pane of frosted glass. That window added a sense of visual space to the tiny chamber, ensured its privacy, and also provided some natural illumination to the enclosed staircase hall. Jacob and Elizabeth and their twelve children needed every one of the six bedrooms; in the interest of economy, most of these were unheated. Like other local farmhouses, the Botz home met fundamental needs without many concessions to comfort.

The family enjoyed socializing, however. A grandson, Paschal Botz, recalled that Jacob and Elizabeth spent hours at a time conversing with visitors about people they mutually knew, whether near or far. Such visiting took place in the *Wohnküche* and in the *Wohnzimmer* (living room), whose chimney-connected stove ensured comfort through the winter months. Images of the Blessed Virgin Mary and the Sacred Heart of Jesus that hung on one wall there also designated the *Wohnzimmer* as a place for family religious devotions, shared at special times of obligation during the Church year. In 1936 Jacob and Elizabeth enjoyed another kind of special time, celebrating their sixty-fifth wedding anniversary in this house.[5] Their life together and tenure on the farm had instilled in the place a tradition of its own.

The Botz house was situated within the farmyard, its kitchen wing pragmatically oriented toward barn and outbuildings. For Jacob and other local farmers, the construction and use of a freestanding dairy barn was, in part, an adaptation to American ways. Parishioners came from an architectural tradition in which peasants and large landholders alike built multipurpose structures in which they lived, sheltered their livestock, and stored their harvest. Niedersachsen Germans had occupied small-scale *Heuerhäuser* or monumental *Hallenhäuser* since the Middle Ages (fig. 4:10). Circumstances

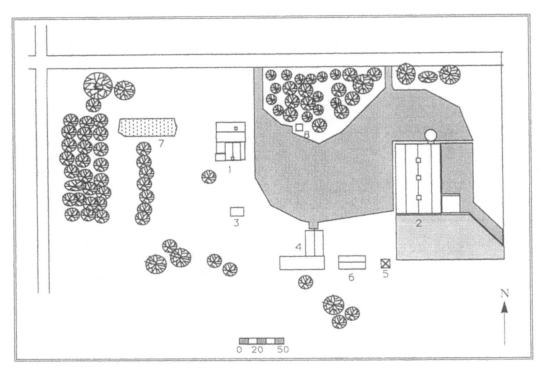

Figure 4:7
Botz farmyard
1. Farmhouse
2. Dairy barn
3. Pump house
4. Granary and machine shed
5. Windmill
6. Calf and heifer shed
7. Kitchen garden
8. Privy

Figure 4:8a
Botz dairy barn, built 1890. The date
plaque is visible over the main doorway.

Figure 4:8b
Floor plan, Botz dairy barn

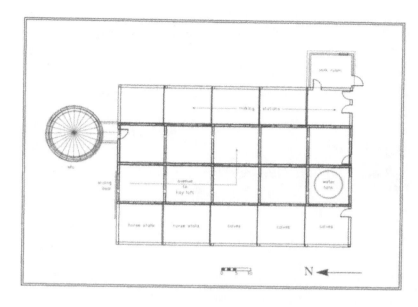

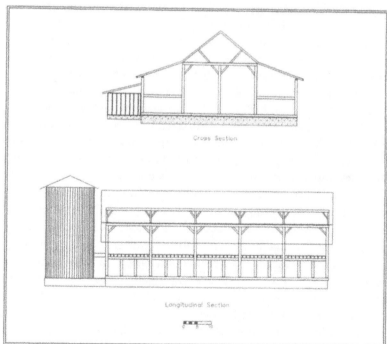

Figure 4:8c
Sections, Botz dairy barn

Figure 4:9
Botz farmyard, 1892

on the Upper Midwestern frontier caused a change from those old ways to new ones: Settlers established themselves on a claim by making separate subsistence shelters for themselves and for their animals. Once the farm developed as a business enterprise able to support new construction, families built structures that would help increase income and provide security. As the most important of these buildings, the barn arose in a space separate from the house.[6]

Jacob and Elizabeth Botz built their cross-wing brick house in 1888 and completed the large dairy barn in 1890. Jacob marked the date in large numerals over the major door to the hay mound (fig. 4:8a). An 1892 photograph of the farmyard (fig. 4:9) shows a fully developed operation. The layout is detailed in figure 4:7. A pump, located over a well and under the windmill, supplied water to the farmyard. A pump house cooled cans of milk in water. Simple, lightweight frame buildings of various sizes and shapes were among the regular features of the farmstead. One or more sheds housed an increasing number and variety of farm implements. A small, compact granary was usually situated near the barn. A swine house and a chicken coop kept the animals that would provide family food staples. A vegetable garden, cultivated in an area just west of the house, was conveniently located near

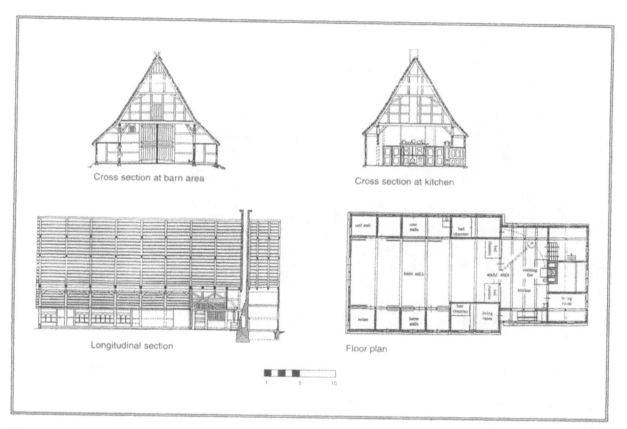

Cross section at barn area

Cross section at kitchen

Longitudinal section

Floor plan

both the kitchen and the outside entrance of the root cellar. The privy was a short walk east.

The 56-by-80-foot barn on the Botz farm was of a type commonly found in areas of German settlement in the Upper Midwest (figs. 4:8a–c). The frame was made of 10-by-10-inch timbers that were mortised, tenoned, and braced at strategic points to form a structure similar to that seen in house-barns of the northwestern German provinces (fig. 4:10).[7] A wide door on the north face of the barn slid open to an L-shaped avenue for horses and wagons hauling hay to the loft. The barn provided stables for work animals and an area for calves and heifers. The stanchions at which the family milked cows were adjacent to the lean-to milk room. Jacob constructed a silo

Figure 4:11a
Henry and Elizabeth Imdieke farmhouse,
Meire Grove, built 1883

adjacent to the barn to store silage for the cows during the months when they could not graze, thus extending milk production through the winter.

Just as the layout of the yard reveals a careful ordering of buildings to facilitate farm chores, the plan and elevation of the Botz barn indicate the remarkable thoroughness with which the structure was conceived and constructed to serve the needs of the dairy operation. The frame was composed of ten central 15-by-13-foot bays bordered by ten side bays, each 15 feet square. This framework was reinforced on the ground level with posts spaced five feet apart in each of the central bays. The 2-by-8-inch joists that helped support the hayloft floor were evenly spaced at 16 inches on center in the central and side bays. Further, the level of the hayloft floor, while a trifle low for the traffic beneath it, was calculated to be optimum for a man moving hay from wagon to loft with a pitchfork. The large door to the central corridor of the barn slid open toward the right; a hinged door would not have functioned in the drifting snow of Minnesota winters. It is evident that Jacob Botz

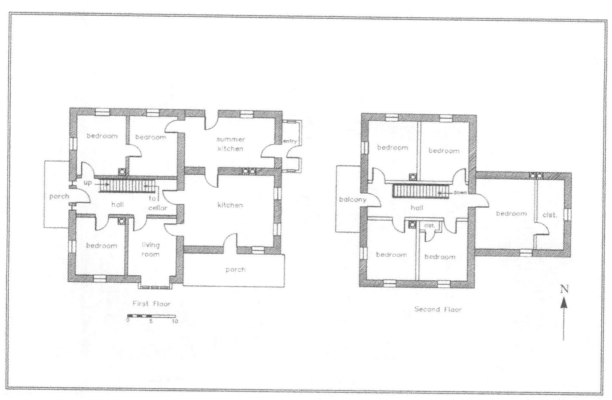

First Floor

Second Floor

N

Figure 4:11b
Floor plan, Imdieke farmhouse

and/or the carpenters who helped him make his barn understood the functions of the structure, knew how to construct a heavy-weight timber frame in a traditional pattern, and also comprehended the details of balloon-frame construction well enough to place members of the frame securely at 16 inches on center. The voices creating the architectural dialogue between the old ways and the new here spoke together with confidence and command.

The cross-wing sections of the 1883 Henry and Elizabeth Imdieke house (figs. 4:11a, 4:11b) appear similar to those of the Midwestern I-house—its name derived from its configuration—a long, narrow two-story unit that is symmetrically divided between central entry and staircase, living room, and dining room. The Daniel Nelson farmhouse (1852–53) in Mahaska County, Iowa, is a regional example of this kind of structure, which was imported to America by English

immigrants (figs. 4:12a, 4:12b). Most Midwestern I-houses include a rear one-story kitchen wing either at one end of the I or at its center.[8] The Imdieke house floor plan indicates a fundamentally different division and use of interior space from that found in the Anglo-American type. The hall-living room wing of this dwelling contained four rooms, not two as in the typical I-house. And instead of the customary ample parlor and dining room or hall, the first floor had three bedrooms and a small rear living room with a bay window. Five more bedrooms were on the second floor. In addition to sheltering a large extended family, the house at times quartered a hired man and two or more nuns who taught in the parish. Eight bedrooms were necessary to accommodate everyone adequately.[9]

The Imdieke house is located across the street from the church in Meire Grove (fig. 2:19). Every Sunday after Mass, some members of the congregation enjoyed socializing before returning to the

Figure 4:12a
Daniel Nelson farmhouse, Mahaska County, Iowa, built 1852–53

Figure 4:12b
First-floor plan, Nelson farmhouse

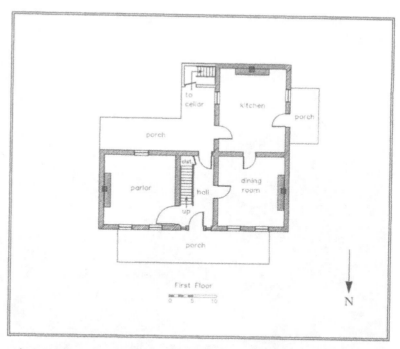

relative isolation of their farm homes. The men adjourned to a local saloon to share a beer and the news. The women walked into the house via the entrance, on Church Street, and either passed through the kitchen to the living room, remained in the kitchen, or, in good weather, relaxed on the porch. The living room was an appropriate focal point for this Sunday gathering because this was where, typically, the family displayed its devotional images.

During the rest of the week, the Imdieke women did their work in the two kitchens, located in the rear wing. A double chimney served a cooking range in each kitchen. Both the summer and central kitchen were places where mother, daughters, and grand-mother prepared and served meals, processed and preserved foods that they stored in the cellar, and cleaned up, pumping water from cisterns beneath each kitchen. They passed to and from their many outdoor chores—tending the vegetable garden, keeping chickens and hogs, and assisting husband and sons in the barn and the fields—via the side portal and rear door.

Figure 4:13
Henry and Elizabeth Imdieke farmhouse
and barn, Meire Grove, ca. 1910 (view
from church grounds)

The house, barn, and outbuildings, like those on the Eveslage farm (fig. 4:5), bordered a central courtyard space; their respective locations emphasized their related functions (figs. 4:13, 4:14). The farmhouse and dairy barn were situated opposite one another on the north-south axis of the courtyard. Smaller outbuildings were strategically located along the east-west axis. Lanes and paths connected all parts of the farmyard, facilitating the family's performance of the daily and seasonal labors of cultivating fields, caring for the animals, and maintaining buildings, machines, and the land itself.

When Henry and local carpenters built the dairy barn, in about 1900, they conceived a structure consisting of five distinct but related units (figs. 4:15a–c). First, they constructed the ground-level framework that acted as a platform for the frame and roof of the

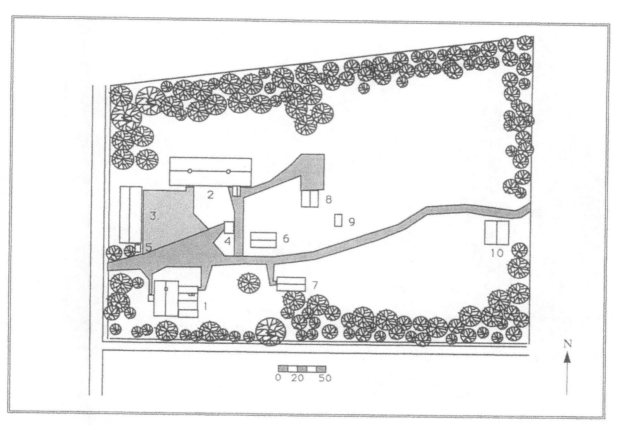

Figure 4:14
Imdieke farmyard
1. Farmhouse
2. Dairy barn
3. Machine shed
4. Privy
5. Windmill and pump house
6. Corn crib
7. Garage
8. Granary
9. Chicken coop
10. Swine house

large hayloft on the second level. Next, they divided the west section of the first level to stable work horses, to house wagons, and to act as a lateral passage for wagons bringing hay to the loft. A large trap door in the passage opened to the loft; it provided ample space for a hook to hoist and carry a load of hay into the space above and drop it at a required distance down the length of the loft. Another trap door, near the east end of the barn, provided a means to pass hay down to the feeding area below, where a row of stanchions comprised a third major unit—the milking stations for as many as sixteen cows.[10] The silo and silage room, situated opposite the stanchions, made up the fourth working area. Last, the milk room, a separate, sanitary space where both milk and cream were processed, was located conveniently near the milking

stations and oriented toward the farm lane in the yard. The mortise-and-tenon frame of the ground level defined a series of central bays, each 9 by 12 feet, balanced by lateral bays that were 12 feet square. The proportions of this 8-foot-high platform were repeated in the loft level, where the framework rose another 24 feet to the central ridge of the gambrel roof. The type of framing used to span and enclose the great space of the structure can be traced to German-American models in Pennsylvania and the Midwest but also directly to framing techniques used in the northwestern German provinces (fig. 4:10).

The Imdieke farmhouse served as shelter for its many occupants, as a place to serve and nourish the family with ample meals at table and good stores in the cellar, as one workplace among many in the rounds of farm labors, as a place to serve social functions for parish members on Sunday, and as a home in which family members, as a group or individually, fulfilled religious obligations of devotions

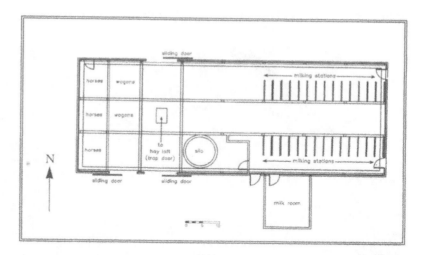

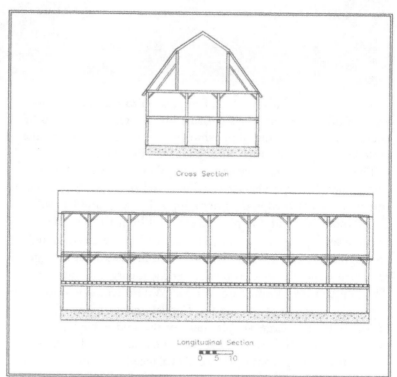

Figure 4:16a
William Brey farmhouse,
Watertown, Wisconsin, built 1847

and prayer. From dawn to dark, from season to season, the duration of life on the farm was measured by the repeated rounds of chores, by the gathering of parishioners every Sunday, and by the cycle of sacramental rituals throughout the liturgical year.

The second general type of brick farmhouse in St. John the Baptist parish is that characterized by a consolidated rectangular or square mass, crowned with either a hipped or a pyramidal roof. The Arnold Nietfeld, Joseph Imdieke, and John Eibensteiner farmhouses (figs. 4:19a, 4:20a, 4:22a) fall within the consolidated-rectangular group. Exterior views of these three structures suggest that their builders modeled them after the Georgian house type. The William Brey farmhouse (1847) in Watertown, Wisconsin, is a vernacular example of this kind of English manor house (figs. 4:16a, 4:16b). The large, simple shape of this end-gable structure generates a sense of massiveness and monumentality. The first story has four large rooms, classically balanced on either side of the formal entrance hall and staircase. The consolidated-rectangular

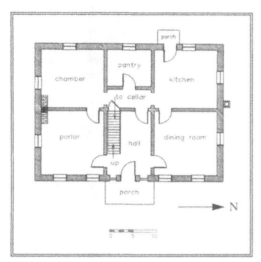

Figure 4:16b
First-floor plan, Brey farmhouse

houses in St. John the Baptist parish do not adhere to this traditional arrangement; they have no entry hall. Rather, in a reflection of characteristic German-American hospitality, their floor plans take the visitor directly into the *Wohnküche.* Formal front entries were seldom used.

Houses of this type derive from similar structures that existed in the villages and towns of the northwestern German provinces. Parishioners re-created versions of these traditional models because they saw such dwellings as expressing the secure socioeconomic position they wished to establish in America. The classically dignified eighteenth-century northern German house seen in figure 4:17 is one such general prototype. Other sources of inspiration were folk renditions of a symmetrically divided rectangular mass, capped by a broad hipped roof, with two lateral chimneys— as in the Bottomsdorf village house of about 1750 shown in figure 4:18. The division of space there is similar to that seen in the German-American examples analyzed here. The placement of staircases and of the lateral chimneys further indicate that specifics of a German model prevailed in the parish farmhouses. This kind of house was the most frequently built there.

Figure 4:17
Elevation, 263 Poppes Landgut, Arsterdam

Figure 4:18
Sections and elevations, farmer's village house, Bottomsdorf, ca. 1750. Clockwise from upper right: front view, longitudinal section, cross section, end view.

Figure 4:19a
Arnold Nietfeld farmhouse, Spring Hill Township, built 1891

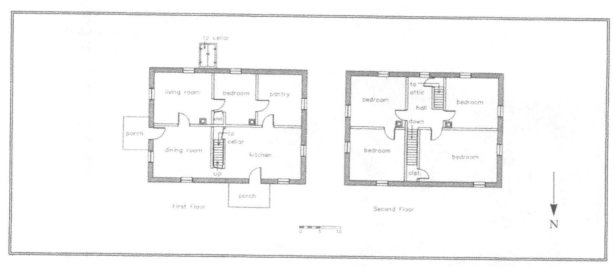

First Floor

Second Floor

N

Figure 4:19b
Floor plan, Nietfeld farmhouse

Figure 4:19c
Cellar floor plan, Nietfeld farmhouse

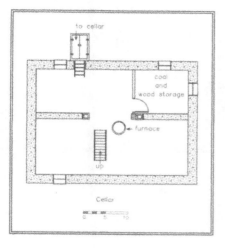

Cellar

Several of Arnold Nietfeld's descendants ascribe the design of his 1891 farmhouse in Spring Hill Township to the parish priest (fig. 4:19a).[11] This attribution seems to be based on the similarity between the shape and massive quality of that structure and the consolidated mass of the church rectories in Meire Grove and other Stearns County parishes. The house also resembles the German models noted above. A half-mile-long lane from the county road takes one to the Nietfeld farmstead, past a large dairy barn, and then to the kitchen entrance on the north side of the house. A front porch once faced another access road. In 1890 that road followed the path of an original Indian trail, which meandered through the area in a southeasterly direction. Second-generation Nietfelds replaced the north and east frame porches with the present brick versions. The relatively light weight of the original frame porches contrasted with and emphasized the simple consolidated brick mass of the main structure. Situated on a rise of land, the house has an impressive monumentality.

On rare occasions, the family would receive guests at the east entrance and usher them into the dining room or living room. The common entrance, as in other parish farmhouses, was the kitchen door. The kitchen and pantry served as a combined working unit.

*Figure 4:20a
Joseph and Elizabeth Imdieke farmhouse,
Grove Township, built 1893*

*Figure 4:20b
Floor plan, Imdieke farmhouse*

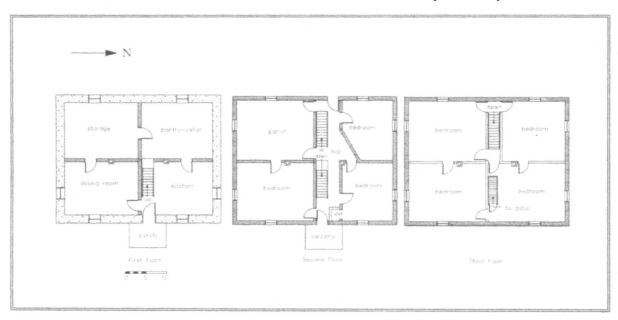

Arnold and his wife probably occupied the small bedroom between the pantry and living room. Four large upstairs bedrooms proved to be ample and comfortable quarters for six Nietfeld children (fig. 4:19b).

The basement, besides providing space for food storage, at one time contained a large homemade furnace (fig. 4:19c). This appliance consisted of a unit for the firebox from which hot air convected through an insulating brick arch. The hot air and the heated brick were to circulate warmth to the first-floor rooms through a large floor opening, covered with an iron grate. When that experiment failed, the two existing lateral chimneys, supported by the central basement wall, were used as the means to pipe the kitchen range and upstairs heating stoves.[12]

Joseph and Elizabeth Imdieke built their 1893 house in Grove Township into the hillside on the farmstead, utilizing what would ordinarily have been basement space as living space (figs. 4:20a, 4:20b). In fact, Frederika Imdieke, who lived there as the wife of one of Joseph's sons, called it "a basement house," recognizing its unusual nature.[13] One entered the kitchen directly at the ground-floor portal on the eastern facade. As in the Nietfeld house, kitchen, pantry, and dining room were grouped together to facilitate the preparation and serving of meals to large families.

A seldom used second-level entry on the west side led to a back parlor and down a hall to three bedrooms. Four more bedrooms on the third floor were sufficient to accommodate the family and its workforce. As was common in the parish, the Imdieke home had many occupants. Besides Joseph and Elizabeth and their nine children, up to four hired men and a servant girl lived there. The men worked in the brickyard in season and as farmhands. The hired girl did many kitchen chores and helped milk the herd of cows that Joseph was developing as he changed the economic basis of the farm operation from cash grains to dairy production and brick manufacture.

The large house, the barn, and other outbuildings are on a slope that descends gently toward the county road (fig. 4:21). After Joseph had nurtured the dairy herd, the major avenue to work was back and forth between the kitchen and the barn. Elizabeth and

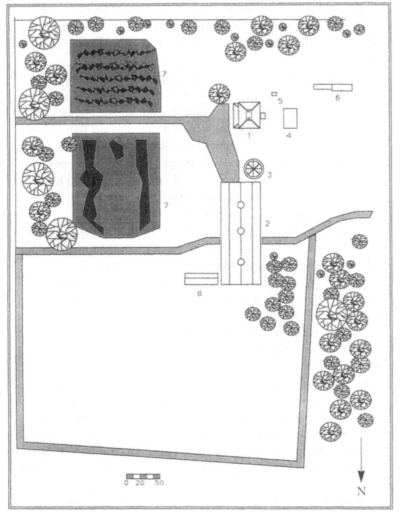

Figure 4:21
Imdieke farmyard
1. *Farmhouse*
2. *Barn*
3. *Silo*
4. *Machine shed*
5. *Privy*
6. *Chicken coop*
7. *Kitchen garden*
8. *Heifer barn*

Figure 4:22a
John and Anna Eibensteiner farmhouse,
Getty Township, built 1904

her daughters cultivated the vegetable gardens, located in protected areas alongside the lane that led to the road. The brickyard developed in a separate but adjacent area south of the house. The stability of the household economy depended upon all these labors and locations functioning together. Family members not only built up the farm and helped operate the brick factory, but they also served important roles in the church parish. Most important, the supply of building materials from the brickyard had a lasting impact on the quality of life for many in the community.

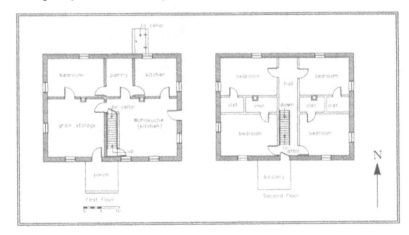

Figure 4:22b
Floor plan, Eibensteiner farmhouse

Figure 4:23a
Elevation, Sears, Roebuck and Company
Glendale model, 1911

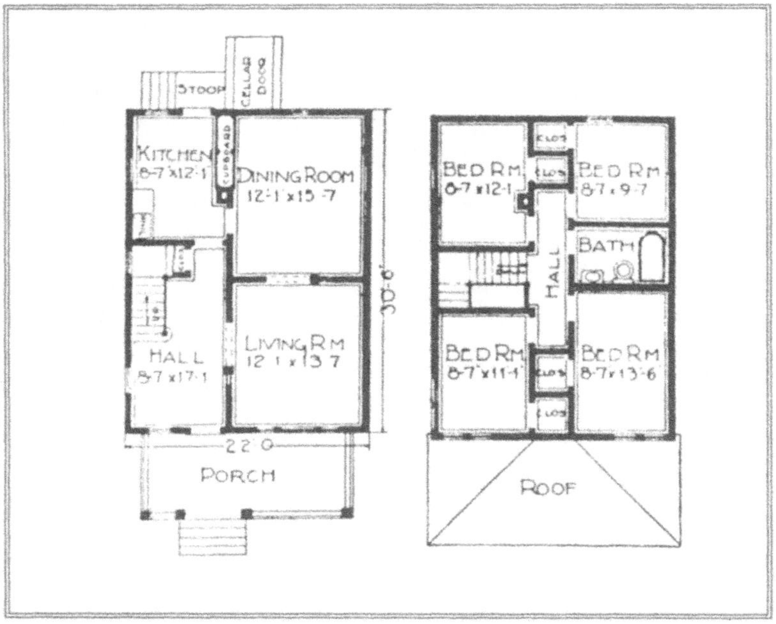

Figure 4:23b
Floor plan, Glendale model

Preference for the rectangular-mass, manorial house type persisted into the early twentieth century, as is reflected in the John and Anna Eibensteiner farmhouse, built in Getty Township in 1904 (fig. 4:22a). The first-floor plan was almost identical to the Nietfeld layout, but the Eibensteiners assigned different functions to the spaces than the Nietfelds did (fig. 4:22b, left). Kitchen, pantry, and the parents' bedroom were aligned at the back of the first floor. One entered the house at a living room/dining room space that functioned as a multipurpose *Wohnküche* in relation to a small kitchen and pantry. The south door was actually an access to a storage room for grain! Here the functions of the farm came directly into the dwelling, as they had in the Niedersachsen *Hallenhäuser*. The second floor was divided by a center hall, flanked by four bedrooms with closets—a design characteristic of other two-story consolidated-type houses in the parish (fig. 4:22b, right). Conveniences included in the basement were the central supporting brick wall and a frame wall that formed a root cellar, shelves on the center wall that provided storage space for canned goods, and a beehive-shaped brick cistern in the northwest corner of the cellar that stored clear soft water for household use.

During the first two decades of the century, some farm families in the parish built brick houses of the consolidated square-mass type (figs. 4:24a, 4:25a). These bear a similarity to the all-American, mass-produced, two-story Foursquare that was popular from the 1890s to the 1920s in city, town, and country as a type that combined utility and efficiency in a low-cost package. The professional architects who designed the Glendale model for Sears, Roebuck and Company organized the rooms of the first floor so that their use would relate to the family and social roles of the house (fig. 4:23b, left). An entry hall allowed one to meet guests formally at the front of the house and visit with them in the adjacent living room. The kitchen was designated as a special-function space at the rear. A dining room that adjoined both the kitchen and living room allowed for convenient service of food to either family or guests. The private family chambers on the second floor included four bedrooms and a bathroom (fig. 4:23b, right).

A comparison of floor plans of the 1904 John and Catherine

Figure 4:24b
Floor plan, Schmiesing farmhouse

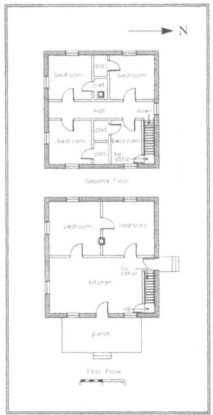

Schmiesing farmhouse in Getty Township with the Sears, Roebuck
Glendale model demonstrates that local design did not follow
these modern plans and behaviors (fig. 4:24b). The traditional
Pfostenwohnhaus division of the first floor into an all-purpose
kitchen and two back rooms centered on the hearth or chimney
appears again. An enclosed staircase to the second floor is tucked
in on the north kitchen wall. The first-floor plan of the 1915
Richard Imdieke farmhouse in Grove Township (fig. 4:25a) is similar, except that the staircase and wall are located near the center of
that house, immediately at the kitchen entrance, allotting space for
a small bedroom next to the kitchen (fig. 4:25b, left). The location
of the staircase in each dwelling does not essentially change a characteristic second-floor arrangement involving four bedrooms of
almost equal size, six closets, and a central hall (fig. 4:25b, right).

Although the Henry and Wilhelmina Haverkamp farmhouse is
of the cross-wing type, the similarity of the floor plan in the square
unit to the *Pfostenwohnhaus* and Schmiesing interiors merits its
inclusion here (fig. 3:8b). Although room designations in the
Haverkamp house differ from those in the Schmiesing and

Figure 4:25a
Richard Imdieke farmhouse,
Grove Township, built 1915

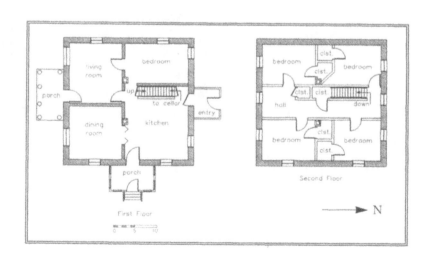

Figure 4:25b
Floor plan, Imdieke farmhouse

Imdieke dwellings, the layout is by now familiar to the reader.[14] The two-story wing extending from the "square" was a farmhouse feature that provided an ample kitchen space downstairs and a dormitory-size bedroom for some of the Haverkamp children upstairs.

It is possible to draw an instructive comparison between a popular American house type and a local German-American type by considering the elevations and floor plans of the Haverkamp and Kind farmhouses. In about 1902, deliveries of Imdieke brick began arriving at a building site in Getty Township, on the southwestern boundary of the parish. The George Kind family, who attended the Lutheran church in nearby Unity, had planned a two-story extended-wing house (fig. 4:26a) that resembled the Haverkamp dwelling. Following what they considered modern principles of design, the Kinds chose a configuration of rooms quite

Figure 4:26a
George Kind farmhouse, Getty Township, built ca. 1902

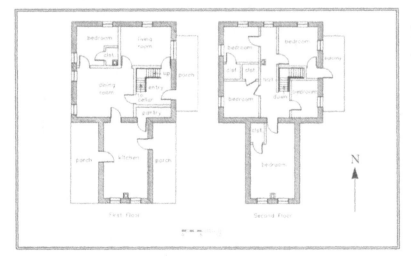

Figure 4:26b
Floor plan, Kind farmhouse

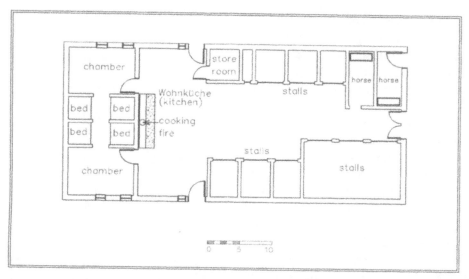

Figure 4:27
Hermann Heinrich Lurding, floor plan for a new house-barn, Northrup, Oldenburg, ca. 1860

similar to those found in the most up-to-date house-catalogue plans. A formal front-entry hall with an open staircase offered passage to both the living room and dining room (fig. 4:26b, left). Locating the kitchen-pantry complex next to the dining room facilitated the serving of guests on special occasions and of the family on an everyday basis.

It is evident that the Kinds did not employ the traditional German-American spatial template when planning the interior of their home. The 18-inch-thick brick walls made the Kind house a Lutheran fortress neighboring the Catholic parish and importing no influence from the many other houses made of Imdieke brick. The walls were tangible cultural barriers that separated the family from the beliefs and values that oriented people of St. John the Baptist parish toward the old ways.

The German-American farmhouses built of Imdieke brick represent only two general types, the cross-wing and the consolidated. Each house type displayed simplicity of shape and demonstrated ease of construction; and each contained an interior that was at once responsive to local requirements and in harmony with ethnic customs for the organizing of domestic space. The German-American template first evidenced in the Zenzen log house (ca. 1870, fig. 2:4b) derived from the traditional *Pfostenwohnhaus* of the northwestern German provinces. The division and use of space in that model and subsequent parish farmhouse interiors was simple and practical. An all-purpose *Wohnküche* centered on the hearth or the heating/cooking range. Two spaces of equal size behind the kitchen served for sleeping and/or storage.[15]

The primary relationship between kitchen and barn had been established in the Niedersachsen *Hallenhäuser*. The correspondence between the first-floor layout of the Schmiesing farmhouse and the domestic space of the German *Hallenhaus* is readily apparent (figs. 4:10, 4:24b, 4:27). In addition to a similar orientation to the barn and a similar division of interior space, stairs are set against walls, providing narrow space with a steep incline to the upper stories. An image recalled, or a quality of space habitually experienced, was operative in the minds of the farm family and builders as they projected the ways the house would function as a familiar and comfortable working place.

The importance of the kitchen, in terms of its size and orientation toward the farmyard, has been repeatedly noted. In many cases, three generations of women—grandmother, mother, and daughters—worked together, perpetuating traditional recipes and rhythms of domestic work. Cooking daily meals for a household of twelve to fourteen was in itself a considerable task. Food preservation involved even larger quantities of edibles—cooked, mixed, and put up for the winter. For instance, one recipe for apple butter called for a barrel of new cider, boiled down by half, and three bushels of peeled, cored good cooking apples. This mixture was to be stirred constantly for eight to ten hours before being cooled and put away in stone jars, sealed with two layers of paper snugly tied down around the lid.[16] Stored on shelves in the cool basement, such a batch would keep a family supplied with this German favorite for months.

Other German-American fare included ample amounts of pickles, sauerkraut, and a mixture of garden vegetables (green tomatoes, cucumbers, green peppers, carrots, cauliflower, green beans, pea pods, and onions) called "pickle pot" or "chow chow." Recipes for these dishes required cups-full and gallons of ingredients. The making of sausage each fall began with the slaughtering of two or more pigs and the butchering, cleaning, and processing of hundreds of pounds of meat and intestines. The final mixture included spices, meal, and cereal. After it was smoked, the sausage would last until the next fall.[17]

The *Wohnküche* always had been and always would be large and central to the operations and well-being of the household and the farm. Parish families who built houses of ample scale followed a traditional division of first-floor space that included a big kitchen and two or more small back rooms. When the kitchen occupied an entire first-floor wing, the space in the central section of the house was used as parlor or living room and bedrooms (fig. 3:8b). When modern domestic amenities became available early in the twentieth century, frugal builders chose not to include or add indoor plumbing to their houses. The old way as the good way, in this case, was the path to the outdoor privy.

That path and all other destinations in the farmyard inevitably led to and from the kitchen door.[18] The location, importance, and function of this portal reflect a social order of family and community in which cooperation in the work of the farm was fundamental and open hospitality to fellow parishioners was assumed. Entering the kitchen of a farmhouse in the parish immediately introduced one to the home's central hearth without the barrier of a formal entry hall at a "front" of the house. Combining entry and domestic functions, a *Flurküche* (entry-kitchen) describes the social function that the *Wohnküche* designation connoted to occupants of the house.[19]

The *Flurküche* reflects community behavior and embodies *social values*. Local precepts of beauty and *aesthetic value* are also related to and derived from these distinctive brick farmhouses of St. John the Baptist parish. Preferences for certain qualities of form and space, decoration, materials, and construction processes will emerge as important factors in the description of the German-American architectural aesthetic that follows.

V

V. BIG, BEAUTIFUL BRICK HOUSES:
A LOCAL AESTHETIC

The Plowman with His
Diligent Hand Produces a
Prosperous Land, *glazed
ceramic tile, n.d.*

German-American farm families and craftsmen built the notable
brick farmhouses of St. John the Baptist parish according to their
aesthetic preferences for qualities of domestic architecture. These
preferences and qualities stemmed from values parishioners shared
about how their environment should look and how things in it
should work. Nobody there wrote a treatise on beauty or penned
an essay on taste, but the community's qualities as a social entity,
ethnic enclave, and religious parish collectively provide sufficient
evidence to enable one to postulate an aesthetic of its architecture.
The history of the parish and features of its built environment
offer means of identifying the values that formed parishioners'
lives and the criteria they used to judge architectural beauty and
excellence. This is not the sort of aesthetic taste that is cultivated
by education and travel but rather is the kind acquired through
practical experience, refined by application and strengthened by
tradition.

An examination of four related ways of interpreting the collective evidence from the parish will help convey a sense of what was
considered the proper "look" to accomplish the necessary "work" of
architecture. First, a general profile of parishioners will be sketched
to delineate character traits that contributed to the building and
maintenance of community, preferences for order and permanence,
and adherence to traditional ways of thought, language, and
action.[1] Second, a discussion of the nature of local building materials and craftsmanship that produced the simple vernacular structures will further an understanding of what parishioners considered
beautiful. Next, a discussion of aesthetic values evident in the
shape, surface, and interior space of parish farmhouses will define

an architectural style that possesses both artistic and ethnic integrity. Finally, a comparison of this local vision of beauty with other trends exemplified in "high-style" architecture of the nineteenth century will complete this definition of the essence of the vernacular aesthetics of St. John the Baptist parish.

A profile of parishioners reveals an industrious group of people who, despite long-term difficulties, were able to establish their farms as enduring agricultural enterprises. In order to help ensure that kind of life, they prized traditional ways that, they believed, would generate order and stability. These beliefs and values were reinforced by their pious participation in the worship and rituals of the Catholic Church (fig. 5:1).[2]

Their slow, persistent development of farmsteads in the competitive economic and technological milieu of nineteenth-century American agriculture indicates a sustained effort to establish a firm

Figure 5:1
Joseph Marthaler family, Grove Township,
ca. 1900

and lasting basis for community. Family name and farm became habitually related as ownership passed from one generation to the next. Acres south of town became known as the Joseph Meyer place; the group of buildings on the spread of land just east of the village made up the J. A. Caspers farm. Farms identified by family name became fixed in the community like stars in a constellation. Parish farmsteads were small in comparison to the more entrepreneurial operations run by members of other ethnic groups in the state and region. Acreage scaled to be operated by the labor-intensive large farm family sufficed to preserve ownership of the homeplace and conserve the resources of the land on which the family depended. Carefully avoiding vulnerability to indebtedness, families cautiously tended the land with hand labor until enough capital was available to enable them to take advantage of improvements made possible by mechanization and scientific techniques for raising crops and caring for livestock. By 1880, farms that had been pioneered in the townships during the late 1850s and the 1860s were sound and profitable; they remained so for generation after generation. Once dairy farming had become the prevailing local occupation, everyone could agree with the following headline in a local newspaper: "Keep up Dairying: In Times of Adversity and Depression the Cow Is the Farmer's Most Reliable Standby."[3] No one grew wealthy in these enterprises, but all residents of the parish benefited from the stability of the farming community as a whole.[4]

When the farms came of age, achievements were substantiated by the built environment parishioners had created—the large, fully appointed church in Meire Grove, substantial homes, large barns and silos, herds of fine milk cows, a dairy cooperative, and commercial enterprises in the village that served those who belonged in and to the community. While these edifices may have appeared to be no different from ones in other rural neighborhoods, they were exclusively those of the individuals, families, and groups who belonged to the congregation of the Church of St. John the Baptist. The experience of creating, sharing, and maintaining this community began and ended with participation in a common religious faith and shared sacred rituals.

Members of St. John the Baptist parish preserved nurturing and protective elements of their inherited folk culture to aid them in founding a community not altogether different from those they had left in the northwestern German provinces. The old ways were maintained in an effort both to preserve meaning from the past and to overcome anxieties and survive in a new, often threatening environment. Landownership and prudent farm practices provided the economic and social conditions in which the accustomed patterns of life could continue.

German was the language of the household, the school, the village businesses, and the church.[5] Use of the native tongue not only sustained familiar means of discourse, but it also perpetuated patterns of thought and expression that were consistent with the nature of life in the parish and of its built environment. German syntax is highly structured; each sentence is built of words and phrases and clauses that fit into their proper places. Whether simple or compound, a sentence has a definite beginning, middle, and end, with the verb frequently placed at the close to complete the statement. The structure of the language demands of the speaker or writer a clear and full conception of a sentence and the interrelationship of its parts before the sentence is begun. Similarly, the dairyman, the carpenter, the brickmason, the kitchen cook sought a comprehensive grasp of the materials, methods, and results of their tasks before judging whether they could begin and satisfactorily finish them. Impromptu performances or efficiencies seemed less important than accomplishing a task carefully and in the right way. This approach was consonant with the order of the language one used to describe and evaluate achievement.[6]

The practical aspects of farm work and village business did not preclude an aesthetic awareness of those labors and the setting in which people performed them. That appreciation focused on a spatial-moral order Germans identified as *die Landschaft*.[7] Traditional meanings of this term denote all aspects of the environment that are cultivated and created from the resources of the earth by means of the skill and ingenuity involved in fine craftsmanship. *Landschaft* connotes the order in which the village, the sacred precincts of the church, the farmsteads, the fields, the pastures, the fence lines, and the roads and lanes are arranged and carefully tended.[8]

Landschaft provided a physical and visual affirmation in the face of the encroaching chaos of nature's destructive forces—the violent storms of every season, the locust plagues of the mid-1870s, and periods of flood or drought. The creation and experience of this kind of protective order constituted a practical and aesthetic achievement shared among generations of parishioners. Once established, this regulated environment satisfied human needs for the proper correlation of meanings in one's world: *Gib dem Boden, so gibt er dir auch.* (What you give to the earth, it will also give to you.) In this context, the built environment can be perceived as a work of art—realized through communal contributions of craft and creative energies and guided by the mutually held values and vision of its makers.

Travel through the parish today presents opportunities to enjoy the various prospects the landscape provides. The hills in the eastern and southern sections offer broad vistas as well as views of meadows framed by oak and poplar. The land in the western portion spreads out toward the prairies north and farther west; its aspect here is open and expansive. The visitor seeks aesthetic categories with which to characterize the experience, but none seems to apply. Picturesque asymmetries and irregularity of form, the order and structure of an ideal image, and sublime vistas are means by which one might understand the land in this part of Minnesota. Yet what this landscape finally communicates are the qualities of care and order. These are not aesthetic qualities; but as exercised by the German-American farm families who have depended upon the land and appreciated its bounty, they produce a kind of pastorale. This place is, however, not an idyllic realm of the past but, as above described, a hard-earned, durable reality.

Diligence, endurance, moderation, protectiveness, piety—such are characteristic traits making up a composite profile of parishioners. Their built environment can be described as small-scale, orderly, well-maintained, and stable. These attributes are reflected in their brick farmhouses.[9]

German-Americans were of course not alone in recognizing the significance of brick. In 1910 the Building Brick Association of America extolled the ancient heritage of the product as "the aristocrat of building materials." Brick also bore qualities of "hospitality, warmth, comfort, beauty. . . [and] is as enduring as the earth itself."[10]

A grandson of Herman Imdieke explained that his grandfather's entry into the brickmaking business in the 1880s was a safe venture because "the settlers arriving from Germany were accustomed to brick houses."[11]

Interviews conducted with old-timers during the late 1980s and early 1990s revealed that their evaluation of local houses was based on the assumption that brick was the appropriate building material; all noted its permanence as a primary quality.[12] For example, ninety-six-year-old Al Imdieke, who had worked in his father's brickyard, remarked that the Caspers farmhouse "looked so nice yet after [one] hundred years."[13] Speaking with authority and from the perspective of an equal number of years, Conrad Nietfeld proudly said of his own house, built in the 1920s, that it "is fifty-three years old and still stands just the way it was."[14] And Frederika Imdieke, who had lived eighty-six years in the parish, aptly summed up the parishioners' forming of their domestic environment as "the building up of big, beautiful brick houses."[15]

The German word for brick is *der Backstein* (baked stone). This alludes to the "alchemy" that transforms mud into stone when dried blocks of clay are burned in the kiln. A lifelong craftsman, writing over a century ago, claimed of the brickmaker that

> *he alone produces the only everlasting, indestructible, and reliable building material on this globe of ours. "Old Time," with his pitiless hand, his remorseless grip, his destroying breath, his ceaseless war, and with endless trophies of victory over all the efforts of man, to withstand his corroding tough and annihilating power, has never been able to destroy a good brick. Every good brickmaker that makes a good brick erects an everlasting monument of his good work.*[16]

In addition to being "everlasting," brick could be enjoyed in both a visual and a tactile manner. When the bricks were set in a wall, their shape and color created a rich and satisfying pattern. The laborer could sense their size and weight as he carried them to the bricklayer, who rhythmically fixed them in place. It would seem that both individuals felt the finished structure to be an extension of their own mental and physical working experience. These elements give substance to the term *das Handwerkskunst* (handwork art, or craftsmanship). Those who appreciated the bricklayer's craft, including neighbors who helped out by hauling bricks to the site, sensed these aspects of construction as they admired both process and product.

The bricklayer was called *der Maurer* (wall-maker). Among local farmers, one criterion of quality for the craft was how readily the bricklayer could set up a wall that stood true and straight and strong, a wall without a single brick out of order. To the accomplished bricklayer, the process came "as easy as eating." An outsider might think that the craft required only mechanical skills. To parishioners, however, *der Maurer* was not only a craftsman but a builder and an architect, too—the one primarily responsible for the construction of a house. He supervised the carpenters and laborers. All work on the structure followed the courses of brick as the walls rose to the height of the roof. Thinking and working in the pattern of his native language, *der Maurer* set up the walls in a way that reflected respect for his craft and a comprehension of the entire structure as well as how the parts related to the whole. The result of his expertise was the shelter and security of the farmhouse.

This study of the aesthetic aspects of brick farmhouses in St. John the Baptist parish is based on analyses of thirty such homes that either remain standing or for which there are photographic records. These dwellings reveal preferences for only two basic house types—the cross-wing and the consolidated—realized in a sober, restrained vernacular form. The structures that best exemplify this aesthetic are: the Henry and Elizabeth Imdieke house in Meire Grove (1883, fig. 5:2a), the Joseph and Elizabeth Imdieke house in Grove Township (1893, fig. 5:2b), the Ferdinand Eveslage house in Spring Hill Township (1885–86, fig. 5:2c), the John and Catherine Schmiesing house in Getty Township (1904, fig. 5:2d), and the Frank and Elizabeth Deters house in Lake Shore Township (ca. 1895, fig. 5:7; see p. 138). A reasonably thorough assessment of the aesthetic qualities of these dwellings is possible because they have been preserved with relatively few alterations or

Figure 5:2a
Henry and Elizabeth Imdieke farmhouse

Figure 5:2b
Joseph and Elizabeth Imdieke farmhouse

Figure 5:2c
Ferdinand Eveslage farmhouse

Figure 5:2d
John and Catherine Schmiesing farmhouse

because they were photographed shortly after being built. One can analyze them as they approximate original conditions and thereby embody the intentions of the families who worked with bricklayers and carpenters to plan and construct them.

A principal trait of each of these representative farmhouses is the simple geometry that describes rectangle and square, defined by broad planar walls. None of the structures has bay windows, towers, or entry halls projecting beyond the main facade. The elevation of each house is firmly defined, either by the broad slope of an end-gabled roof or by the protective crown of a hipped roof. Devoid of brackets or bargeboards, the rooflines clearly mark the division between the massive substructure and the frame roof. Wooden frame porches do not conceal the substantial facades from which they extend. Typically, the porches face the farmyard and not the country road, indicating that any decorative flair added to a house was not for public display of socioeconomic status or refined taste.

Conceiving of these houses mainly in terms of their interior spaces, builders enclosed familiar, traditional floor plans within elemental architectural masses. These farmhouses amplify the shapes that define the cross-wing and the consolidated type through the solidity and firmness of brick and mortar. Parish families' selection of these types seems to have been based on their adaptability to specific design needs and satisfaction of aesthetic preferences for simplicity and stability. Whatever element of fashion or prestige might generally be associated with the given house type was subordinated to what looked good and worked well in the context of the family and the community.

The aesthetic inherent in basic shapes and types of these farmhouses applied to their exterior surfaces as well. The houses were constructed of common brick from the Imdieke factory; no special face brick was produced there. Specific features of some of the houses and general traits they all share indicate ways in which masons integrated decorative elements into the outside brickwork. Each corner of the Jacob and Elizabeth Botz house in Getty Township, for instance, is visually strengthened by pillarlike projections from the wall and corbeled-brick course-work at the eaves and on the foundation line (fig. 4:6a). A similar articulation was

Figure 5:3a (left)
*Window head, Joseph and Elizabeth
Imdieke farmhouse*

Figure 5:3b (middle)
*Window head, Henry and Elizabeth
Wehlage farmhouse*

Figure 5:3c (right)
Window head, Arnold Nietfeld farmhouse

used on the Ferdinand Eveslage farmhouse. This elaboration creates the impression that the walls are supported by a massive columnar framework, structurally reinforced at the foundation and roofline. The shadows cast by the corner pillars and projecting brick beneath the eaves visually define the walls and further emphasize the shape of the structure itself.

Windows and doors placed at regular intervals generate steady rhythmic movement across the farmhouses' broad, planar exterior walls. That rhythm is accented by window heads—the courses of brick that project from and arch over each window. Besides creating a restrained decorative effect, they perform the practical function of diverting rainwater and condensation from the wooden window frames.[17] The variety of examples seen in the houses discussed here displays the inventiveness of the brickmasons, who suited patterns to each house. But whether formed by two or more courses of low arching brick extending from the wall in low relief (fig. 5:3a), set as an arch with dentils (fig. 5:3b), or forming an arch with consoles (fig. 5:3c), each window head is subordinated to the surface of the wall and proportions of the overall structure.

The brickmason also varied the textural appearance of the exterior

Figure 5:4a (left)
Beaded brick joint, Joseph and Elizabeth
Imdieke farmhouse

Figure 5:4b (right)
Flush brick joint, Arnold Nietfeld farmhouse

walls with the finish he applied to the mortar joints. Two finishes affecting the shadow line between bricks are evident in parish farmhouses. The *beaded joint* finishes flush with, and sometimes slightly beyond, the surface, creating a light shadow line and giving the wall a relatively smooth look (fig. 5:4a). The bricklayer made a *flush joint* by maintaining the level of mortar at the surface of the brick (fig. 5:4b). The bands of mortar between bricks appear broader than in the beaded joint, making the bricklaying pattern more clearly visible. The flush joint also highlights the proportioned structural qualities of the wall by outlining every component. The firmness of the granite foundation visually reinforces the strength of the brick wall above.

Figure 5:5
Brick house with corner pillars and corbeled
brick, Dinklage, Oldenburg, Germany, 1990

In addition to its other characteristics, brick changes in color and texture over time. A brick wall does not look the same ten years after construction. This long-term process was observed and enjoyed as a positive, pleasing quality: The brick endured and had a history. It matured, as did the occupants of the home.

Parishioners' preferences for simple geometry, moderate decoration, and durable materials derived from their ethnic background. Formed and sustained by their traditions, these German-Americans maintained a remarkable amount of the vocabulary of an Old World architectural language in both the outsides and insides of their houses. Those who planned and realized brick dwellings perpetuated a choice of material that everyone in the parish shared. When asked why parishioners built houses of brick, Frederika Imdieke pounded the table and shouted, "Bricks!" The answer was in the question. Tradition assumed structures made of *der Backstein*.

The practices of creating corner-pillar accents and adorning wall surfaces with various window heads and brickwork patterns stem from the craft traditions of the northwestern German provinces (fig. 5:5). Some parish farm families emulated another homeland

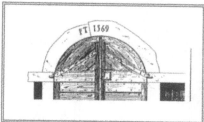

Figure 5:6a (top)
Inscribed stone name-date plaque, wealthy farmer's house, Grosz-Ottersleben, 1785

Figure 5:6b (middle)
Inscribed stone name-date arch, Kr. Mosbach farmhouse, Binau, 1569

Figure 5:6c (bottom)
Inscribed stone name-date plaque, Henry and Wilhelmina Haverkamp farmhouse, 1899. See also figure 3:8a.

custom by setting a stone or cement plaque bearing their name and the year the house was built on the second story of the principal brick facade. The owners of large farms in Niedersachsen had placed such plaques on the lintels of their great house-barns (figs. 5:6a, 5:6b), and burghers likewise marked their urban houses, especially those whose scale and style bespoke prestige. In St. John the Baptist parish, name-date plaques served to herald the achievement of newfound status in America (fig. 5:6c).

Local builders produced interior domestic spaces that were arranged and utilized in ways similar to those they and their forebears had known in Oldenburg and Westphalia. They creatively adapted the substance of what they remembered from the Old World to the skills they were learning and the knowledge they were acquiring in the New World. Evidence of this transfer and adaptation appeared first in the German-type cabins that many pioneers built (fig. 2:2). Construction of the first log church in Meire Grove was based on Niedersachsen techniques employing raw materials to achieve a simple, moderately scaled edifice (fig. 2:6). The layout of some of the early frame houses in the parish bore a remarkable likeness to the traditional division and use of rooms, which revolved around a central hearth (figs. 2:4b, 2:5, 2:10). The floor plan of virtually every brick farmhouse exhibits a variation on this basic spatial template, recalled from the *Pfostenwohnhäuser* and the *Hallenhäuser* of the northwestern German provinces.[18] The frequency with which the template appears indicates that its application to new situations was neither accidental nor random; clearly, it satisfied parishioners' partiality for a certain familiar quality of domestic space. The heritage of this floor plan resonated with ethnic as well as aesthetic significance.[19]

Correspondences between parishioners' character traits and the architectural qualities they preferred is evident. These relationships are basic to a concept of style in which salient and recurring features of works of art reflect the temperament of the individual or group who created them. The presence of style in performance is also a measure of aesthetic quality insofar as style reflects a coherent, significant expression of meaning.

A comparison of the Frank and Elizabeth Deters home (fig. 5:7) with an Anglo-American and a Norwegian-American farmhouse of similar shape and scale will clearly illustrate the architectural aesthetic of St. John the Baptist parish in relation to other contemporaneous vernacular preferences. Each of the three houses is a large, almost square two-story unit with a projecting, narrower two-story wing. Given this compositional similarity, one can discern how each representative structure makes an architectural statement about form and decoration.

The Anglo-American farmhouse, built in western Ohio's Miami County in about 1880, is constructed of brick (fig. 5:8). The ornamentation on its principal facade expresses the owner's and builder's knowledge of fashionable decorative features, gathered

Figure 5:7
Frank and Elizabeth Deters farmhouse,
Lake Shore Township, built ca. 1895

Figure 5:8
Eclectic-style brick farmhouse, Miami
County, Ohio, built ca. 1880

from architectural stylebooks. The simplicity of the hipped roof
contrasts with the amount and variety of ornament below it—an
elaborate cornice whose relief patterns of intertwined braid are reg-
ularly divided by double brackets. The decorative two-story porch
visually unifies the facade by extending the plane of the larger unit
across both units. The front door is placed left-of-center in its section to further the appearance of a broad and balanced facade. The
segmented window heads are crowned with a cartouche of braided
line, enriched by dentils, and finished with consoles. The window
sills are divided into two volumes and supported by brackets at
each end. The doorway is given a similarly elaborate treatment,
functioning as a special focus with transom and side lights that
increase its height and width. Window scale and proportion also

Figure 5:9
Lars L. Quaal farmhouse, Lac qui Parle
County, built ca. 1895

vary—from the tall, slender form on the first story to the short, broad fenestration on the second. Pillars with complex bases and elaborate capitals support the porch on both levels. The banister exemplifies the jigsaw wizardry of the nineteenth-century carpenter.

The aesthetic statement of the Ohio farmhouse is sophisticated and complex. So many stylistic languages speak at the same time. Elements of Georgian and Federal styles, of neo-Gothic, and Italianate designs mix with Victorian bric-a-brac.[20] Yet while the house has delightful qualities and decorative flair, it fails to achieve a cohesive syntax—a core of meaning and tradition from which to communicate.[21]

The decoration of the house that the Norwegian-American Lars L. Quaal built in Lac qui Parle County, Minnesota, in about 1895 (fig. 5:9) is not as exuberant or ostentatious as that of the Ohio farmhouse. Still, it is evident that Quaal wanted to impress neighbors with a display of taste and economic achievement. Like the veneer of brick that wraps the frame house, ornamental features seem applied to the surface rather than integrated into its design. Ironwork along the crest of the roof and in the railing on the balcony over the veranda introduce lacy two-dimensional linear patterns to the decor. Dark wooden brackets contrast with courses of light brick under the eave. Window heads repeat this rhythm of surface contrasts. The front porch, bay window, and veranda further elaborate the facade with spindles, shingles, and contrasting patterns of color.

There is a kind of restraint expressed in the Quaal house; its show of wealth and position draws attention but is not overbearing. Other farmhouses in Quaal's Norwegian-American neighborhood were framed and ornamented in wood (fig. 3:9a). The brick surface may distinguish his home from the others, but the substantial veneer resembles a decorative coating of shiplap.

By contrast, the German-American aesthetic manifested in the Deters farmhouse makes a direct statement about vernacular simplicity. The structure does this without pretending to be anything other than what it is—a well-conceived, skillfully executed structure. The facades of both its units are relatively unadorned. Each is balanced by the regular placement of windows, with simple ornamental heads. The spindle-work decorative dormers on the roof mark each center and strengthen the symmetry of the two units. Spindle-work ornament also enlivens the two frame porches but does not obscure the shape and scale of either. The scale of the entire structure and proportion of its pair of units, as well as its windows, doors, and porches, contribute to its clarity of form and integrity.[22]

The home manifests representative features of the local architectural style. Brick construction appears as an embodiment of the endurance of the Deters farm family, posed in front of their home (fig. 5:7). They form a line as straight and true as the courses of bricks in the walls of their dwelling. These are the folk characterized as hardworking, tenacious, conservative, protective, and pious. The house and the family alike are orderly, stable, and permanent. The shape, surface, and plan of the house are of simple vernacular form. Its exterior ornamentation bespeaks a domestic environment that, like its occupants, lacks ostentation or affectation. The layout of interior spaces recalls the familiar dwellings of the northwestern German provinces. The family and craftsmen together created a structure that satisfied priorities for these formal and traditional qualities. Fulfilling these aesthetic criteria, the Deters home and the other "big brick houses" of St. John the Baptist parish were, indeed, perceived and experienced as strong, secure, and beautiful. *Jawohl, sie sind so schön!*

VI

Feast of Corpus Christi
Procession *(detail), engraving,*
1894

VI. RURAL PIETY:
FAMILY, FARM, AND CHURCH

The Catholic Church helped situate German immigrants in central Minnesota and cared for their spiritual well-being as they struggled to establish farms. The Church of St. John the Baptist and membership in its congregation were of fundamental importance to the growing community. Parishioners believed that the spiritual power of the Church was necessary not only for salvation but also for obtaining blessings in this life. Parish homes were places of family worship—stages for the performance of religious rituals and enactment of sacramental rites. Through these means and in these settings, parishioners believed, the priest channeled sustaining grace from the church to the home and farm. That transfer of power provided an ultimate security against the vicissitudes of temporal life and the difficulties and dangers of farming in central Minnesota. In addition to its role as an integral working unit of the farm, the home was a sanctified environment in parishioners' lives. The substantial nature of the house as structure and the religious quality of the home as sacred overlapped and bonded together.

Parishioners all shared in the experience of being nurtured by the Church through its sacraments and sacramentals. Religious education about the meaning of the sacraments was the fundamental ground from which clergy developed a rural piety appropriate to parish families' daily lives. The local church worked "towards the introduction, inculcation, progress in, and reinforcement of the Catholic faith upon the individual, so as to make him [or her] an integral, steadfast, component of the system."[1]

Within a month after a child's birth, parents and sponsors brought the baby to receive the sacrament of Baptism, the initiatory rite that enabled one to receive other sacraments. This ritual

Figure 6:1
First Communion, Church of St. Augusta,
St. Augusta, Minnesota, ca. 1910

Figure 6:2
Confirmation class, Church of St. Joseph,
St. Joseph, Minnesota, ca. 1927

Figure 6:3
The Seven Sources of Grace, *engraving,*
1894

cleansing with water also introduced the infant into the care of the congregation of St. John the Baptist. Virtually everyone in this small community observed the behavior of others. Parents and elders watched children and young adults as part of a process of social control and collective tutoring in the ways of the world and the path to salvation. Children began receiving religious education at home and at church while still quite young. At age six or seven, boys and girls were able to participate fully in the Mass upon receiving the sacraments of Penance and the Eucharist (Holy Communion) (fig. 6:1). Formal religious education continued until young people received the sacrament of Confirmation and became adult members of the church (fig. 6:2).[2] The sacrament of Matrimony (marriage) further integrated husband and wife into the organization and social life of the parish by qualifying them as members of the men's Verein (the Saint Joseph's Society) and the Christian Mothers Society (the Saint Mary's Society).[3] From the celebration of First Communion to the moment one received the sacrament of Extreme Unction before death, the individual was expected to be a faithful participant in the Eucharist. Ideally, one could attend Mass every day, but solemn obligations were more realistically mandated for Sunday Mass and certain Holy Days of Obligation throughout the Church year.[4]

As visible signs of an invisible grace, the Seven Sacraments provided the religious framework and spiritual sustenance, enabling individuals to meet their moral obligations and participate in parish life (fig. 6:3). The sacraments linked the human and the divine. The priest controlled these means of grace as he administered them to parishioners in the church. Sacraments performed there invoked God's presence in a special way.

According to Church dogma, Christ ordained the sacraments. But the Church instituted sacramentals as means of petitioning God to bestow his blessings on places and in situations where believers lived and labored.[5] The priest officiated at sacramental rituals that relayed blessings to the farm family's environment and offered spiritual power to meet the various needs and concerns of farming. Sacramentals involved not only ceremonies, such as public processions, but also material substances or objects, for example, water, statues, or candles. The nature and import of sacramental rites were rooted in symbol and metaphor, insofar as they related two levels of experience and meaning. The clergy who administered these rites and the laity who participated in them believed in the existence of an invisible connection between the material world and the spiritual one—a connection directly expressed through the sacramental.

The pious believed that water became holy when blessed in the church. In this spiritually potent state, the substance could transmit blessings to whomever or upon whatever it was administered. One experiences water in and of itself as essential to health. In other contexts, water symbolizes the origins of life. When holy water is used in a sacramental act, the metaphorical relation of physical washing to spiritual cleansing introduces another dimension of meaning.[6] As one German-American Benedictine monk explained:

> *Man requires signs and ceremonies to impress him. It is a natural tendency. He seeks for symbols in nature, he speaks and acts metaphorically, and attaches to things a moral meaning. Not being a pure spirit, he can raise his mind to spiritual things only by means of things created and visible. Long ago the Church realized that she must speak in the language of the multitude. . . . Our wise Mother the Church takes men where they are and speaks to them of what they know.*[7]

The celebration of Rogation Days illustrates basic qualities of sacramentals as ritual. On the Monday, Tuesday, and Wednesday preceding Ascension Thursday, the priest and parishioners formed a procession that followed routes through Meire Grove to nearby cropland on either the Imdieke or the Meyer farm. The congregation and choir chanted litanies and recited prayers of penance, seeking God's mercy. The priest asked God to bless the fruits of the earth as he sprinkled fields, gardens, and orchards with holy water. One prayer said during the procession read:

> We beg of Thy goodness, O Almighty God, that the fruits of the earth which Thou dost deign to nourish by means of temperate breezes and rain, may be penetrated by the dew of Thy blessings; grant also to these people who ever thank Thee for Thy gifts; that the fertility of the earth may enrich the hungry with an abundance of good things.[8]

Recited in May near planting time, the litanies of Rogation Days were vitally important to these farm families.[9]

The parish priest and congregation celebrated sacramental rituals and parish festivals throughout the liturgical year that, like Rogation Days, related the work of the church to the labors of the farm. These occurred at crucial times of planting, cultivation, and harvest of crops and care of livestock. As a cycle of celebrations, they responded in due season to families' concerns and supported their work. The priest officiated at frequent Masses and sacramentals during spring planting. On April 4 he celebrated the Mass of St. Isadore, a patron saint of agriculture. In that service he offered special prayers to help ensure good crops in the coming growing season and blessed seeds and grain that farmers brought to the sanctuary. Families returned home from Palm Sunday services with palm fronds that the priest had blessed (fig. 6:4). Parishioners believed these fronds conveyed new spiritual life to the home and farm; they replaced last year's palms—tacked over the dining-room door, nestled behind the holy pictures

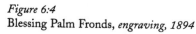
Figure 6:4
Blessing Palm Fronds, *engraving, 1894*

in the living room, or nailed over the barn door.[10] As parts of a tree that symbolized victory over Satan and his forces of evil, fronds were seen to have power to protect homes and fields against the destructive forces of nature.[11] When a severe storm approached, a family member burned a segment of the frond as a further gesture to ward off danger.[12]

Water blessed at the Mass of Holy Saturday before Easter was another spiritually imbued substance used in the home all year. The faithful believed it cleansed one of venial sin and also expelled evil spirits and physical diseases.[13] Families brought containers of holy water from the church to their homes. They kept some in their bedrooms so they could bless themselves with it at morning and evening prayers.

Figure 6:5
Blessing Bread, *engraving, 1894*

The blessing each night was to see them through hours of darkness, which, once all candles or kerosene lamps had been extinguished, was deep and sometimes overwhelming. During stormy nights especially, the darkness seemed absolute. At such times, parishioners often sprinkled holy water inside or around the outside of the house to help protect it from the threatening weather.[14]

On Easter Sunday, celebrants of the Resurrection brought grain and home-baked bread to Mass so that the blessing of the church connected the new life of the risen Christ with the life and labors of hearth and field (fig. 6:5). On April 25, a date that usually falls after Easter, parishioners had another opportunity to pray for a successful year as they celebrated the Mass of St. Mark the Evangelist, a protector of the farmer. This mass preceded the litanies of Rogation Days.

The Feast of Corpus Christi, which followed Trinity Sunday in June, involved all congregants in a devotional event focused on the Eucharist. After tolling bells called parishioners to church, the priest said a High Mass. Leaving the sanctuary after this solemn service, they were greeted by the parish band, which led them in musical procession to the cemetery just east of the church (figs. 6:6a, 6:6b). The procession was formed in units according to age and hierarchy of church organizations and societies. While reciting

Figure 6:6a
Feast of Corpus Christi procession, Church
of St. Augusta, June 11, 1914

Figure 6:6b
Feast of Corpus Christi procession, Church
of St. Augusta, June 11, 1914

the Rosary, a cross-bearer, acolytes, children, and adults followed the priest to four small frame buildings or arbors located at each corner of the cemetery. Every arbor contained an altar and holy objects and images relating to the Passion of Christ. In front of each arbor, the priest performed an appropriate Benedictine service. The feast concluded when the procession returned to the sanctuary for a liturgy and benediction.

The Feast of Corpus Christi involved all members of the congregation working together. Designated families gave special care to the preparation and decoration of the four arbors. The band practiced its part in the ceremonies. The sacred service connected to farm labors through the following blessing, which extended beyond the participants to all of nature: "Even inanimate nature commemorates its redemption. For the flowers in their brightness, the fields in their verdure, the trees in their blossoms, the birds in their singing, the day in its freshness and beauty, all seem to unite with devout Christians in praising and giving thanks."[15]

The German-American Catholics of St. John the Baptist parish linked the Feast of Corpus Christi with *Kranzeltag* (Day of Wreaths)—a folk celebration from the northwestern German provinces held at the same time—part of which involved the offering of prayers to protect and bless newly planted crops. Frederika Imdieke's mother incorporated a custom she recalled from that homeland festival into the Corpus Christi observance: Over the walk to the main church portal she and other women constructed two arches of greenery, under which the procession passed on its way to and from the sacramental rites at the cemetery arbors.[16] This blending of a folk practice into a religious ceremony connected the power of the Mass to the fertility of the earth and to the central concerns of the local farm families.[17]

The daylong *Erntdankfest* (Harvest Festival), held in September, was a combined sacramental and social event. In the morning the priest offered a High Mass, after which began the annual parish bazaar. An auction of items that congregation members had made to benefit the parish and its missions was the main social feature of the day. The festival provided a time for families to celebrate after completing the year's cycle of planting, cultivation, and harvesting labors.

Just as the farm families accomplished rounds of chores each day and month, the parish priest performed sacramentals in due season. Besides officiating at communitywide ceremonies and festivals, the priest visited farms to administer blessings to families, their work, and their homes. For example, he was invited to bless a new house when it was ready for habitation. Members of the extended family, friends, and neighbors joined the ceremony, all following the priest as he bestowed upon each room an appropriate prayer and a sprinkling of holy water. Standing before the main entrance—the kitchen door—he prayed:

> *O God, make the door of this house wide enough to receive all who need human life and fellowship, narrow enough to shut out all envy, pride, and strife. Make its threshold smooth enough to be no stumbling-block to children, nor to straying feet, but rugged and strong enough to turn back the tempter's power. God, make the door of this house the gateway to your eternal kingdom.*[18]

With this prayer the kitchen door, which opened onto the farmyard, became a portal not only toward daily labors but also toward one's salvation.

The celebration of Rogation Days, noted above, further strengthened the link between the secular and the sacred, bringing the priest to parish farms to sanctify and hence spiritually empower buildings, animals, produce, grain, fields, and tools. By means of this sanctification, parishioners believed, the barn became a hallowed place, the herd of dairy cows consecrated creatures, and the land ready for the service of the farm family, the parish, and God.

Candles consecrated during Candlemas, celebrated on the Feast of the Purification of the Blessed Virgin Mary on February 2, became special tapers used for family devotions in the living room or when circumstances necessitated that the priest administer Extreme Unction at home. When severe summer storms or winter blizzards threatened the house and farm, family members lit these candles to ward off danger. Burning at the center of the kitchen table or on a stand in the living room, the flickering, dancing candlelight illuminated drafty chambers in the midday darkness that accompanied turbulent weather. More than a common taper, these sanctified lights furnished spiritual security and comfort.

The priest blessed other objects parishioners employed in their devotional lives. Individuals asked the priest to hallow rosaries, missals, medals, and the holy statues or pictures that became shrines within the home. According to Catholic piety, use of these items in sacramentals and devotions was effective in obtaining the spiritual merit or grace that the Church attributed to various acts of prayer and worship.

Every family member possessed his or her own rosary beads and used them daily. One or more sets of beads marked the places in the home where an individual or the family performed devotions; they could be hung from hooks or brackets on kitchen, living-room, or bedroom walls. Each segment of the rosary beads led believers through an established series of prayers and meditations upon the mysteries of the faith. Kneeling at bedside or at a living-room chair, those who said the Rosary began with the small crucifix appended to the string of beads by reciting the Apostles' Creed, followed by an Our Father (the Lord's Prayer), three Hail Marys, and a doxology (or Glory Be to God). After a meditation on the first mystery of the Annunciation, one prayed ten Hail Marys and a doxology before proceeding to the second mystery of Mary visiting Elizabeth, an Our Father ("Vater Unser. Der du bist in Himmel. Geheliget werde dein Name. Zu uns komme dein Reich" [Our Father who art in Heaven. Hallowed be Thy Name. Thy kingdom come]) and ten Hail Marys ("Gegrüszest seist du, Maria. Voll der Gnade. Der Herr is mit dir" [Hail to you, Mary. Full of grace. The Lord is with you]). The German addressed these prayers in the familiar *du* (you), making the petitions more immediate and personal. The daily devotions at home established tangible ties with the spiritual realm that were directly efficacious in this life and the next. Indulgences of a specified nature—for instance, time released from Limbo or Purgatory or intervention for special causes—could be earned by reciting a Rosary. Families also recited the Rosary together in the living room to protect themselves and their farm during especially stormy nights.[19] The stark flashes of lightning and the crescendo of thunder from a storm front carrying heavy rain and hail across fields and pastures set a frantic rhythm in which the family prayed: "Heilige Maria, Mutter Gottes. Bitt für uns, arme Sünder, jetz und in der Stunde unseres Todes." (Hail Mary, Mother of God. Pray for us sinners, now and at the time of our death.)

During the second half of the nineteenth century, the Catholic Church hierarchy encouraged parish priests to foster a new, more standardized form of devotions to replace local customs that focused on particular saints and shrines. The Church supported the use of authorized and sanctified rosaries, medals, and images in recitation of the Rosary, novenas, confessions, and other prayers. Both the new and the traditional devotions assumed that a social relationship could be established between the pious Catholic and a supernatural being, a saint, to whom the individual addressed petitions. This kind of interaction created a sense of intimacy and divine protection in the life of the faithful as they continually turned to divine intercession to affect earthly matters.[20]

The parish priest and Church hierarchy continually encouraged the pious to adhere to a regular round of devotions. The day began with morning prayer and ended with evening prayer. While at work, one meditated upon God's grace, upon the Blessed Virgin Mary, or upon the meaning of Christ's sacrifice. In order to attain a perfect piety, one was to seek purity of heart, conscience, and action. Equally significant was the outward demeanor and behavior of the pious. One was to practice modesty and simplicity in clothing and living environment, to be regular in one's daily labor, rest, and meals. Devotional books guided each day of the week in a particular kind of reverence toward the Holy Angels, the Seven Sacraments, and the Holy Trinity.[21] St. John the Baptist parishioners had already created this kind of life and practiced this kind of discipline in their daily and seasonal farm labors. Christian piety appeared to them as a practical, yet spiritual, extension of what was already required of a responsible and successful animal husbandman.

The foregoing explanation of sacraments, sacramentals, devotions, and duties has sketched in general terms how clergy and laity created close, abiding connections between the sanctuary of the church, the shelter of the home, and the vocation of farming. A more concrete understanding how pious practice related church and home can be gained by considering the lives of one large parish farm family in particular.

Jacob and Elizabeth Botz were wed through the sacrament of Matrimony in 1872. Working together on their farm in Getty Township, they were able to increase its size from 160 acres in 1872 to 280 acres in 1895. By that time, they had nine children; three others had died. Some of the children were old enough to help with the kitchen, barn, and field chores. In addition to fulfilling the obligations of Sunday worship during the Church year, the Botz family also celebrated the baptism, penance and communion, confirmation, and marriage of their children as they matured to adulthood. The ordination of Jacob and Elizabeth's son Paschal to the priesthood was an especially significant event. The family also witnessed Extreme Unction and participated in funeral ceremonies for the three children who had died. Besides marking these spiritual milestones, they took part in a similar round of observances, celebrations, and mournings with members of their extended family and with friends and neighbors. Further, they joined in the various sacramentals and blessings of the Church year. Among these, the priest's visit to the farm during Rogation Days was an especially important annual occasion.

Like other homes in the parish, the Botz farmhouse was a place for family and individual devotions. Grace and prayer at mealtimes in the kitchen were constants. Appropriately, a picture of the Last Supper hung in this room. Each night during Lent the family recited the Rosary together in the living room, where images of the Blessed Virgin Mary and the Sacred Heart of Jesus comprised a devotional shrine, illuminated with candles that the priest had blessed. Kitchen chairs arranged in a circle in the living room became impromptu kneeling benches for the observance of these solemn rituals. The family scheduled times to perform these and other devotions to fit within the tightly organized daily round of labors that were inherent in life on a dairy farm.

One is tempted to tally the number of religious services and ceremonies the Botz family attended and thus quantitatively measure the extent to which each of them was involved in the interconnections among church, house, and farm. A qualitative evaluation would be more appropriate: a narrative that relates the day-to-day, season-to-season, year-to-year blending of the sacred and secular aspects of life in the experience of the Botz family.[22]

The pious Catholic life, it is said, is learned not only through the study of text and memorizing of catechism passages; it is passed down and experienced through the splendor of the sanctuary—the scents of incense and burning candles, the feel of water, oil, cloth, rosary beads, the taste of the Eucharistic wafer, the music of the pipe organ, and the ringing of the steeple bells. The rural piety nurtured by the Church of St. John the Baptist extended the palpable experience of faith beyond the sanctuary to the domestic realm, where aromas from the kitchen and even the odors of the farmyard transmitted qualities of religious life to the next generation.[23]

The sacraments sanctified life, and the sacramentals that extended that grace to home and work provided the German-American Catholic farmer a framework within which to strive toward salvation in the next life while also negotiating the terms of his situation in this one. Pious observance of the means of grace, rites, and rituals offered hope not only for an eternal reward but also for significant recognition from God and an extraordinary acknowledgment of one's piety. Although the farm family might feel physically secure in a brick house recently blessed by the parish priest, the work of plowing the earth, sowing the seed, cultivating the crop, and reaping the harvest was perpetually risky. Putting hand to plow meant entering into a bargain with nature to work with and accept the conditions allotted in the given season. Putting hand to scythe involved the landsman in an assessment of the fortune gained or lost in the gamble. The husbandman experienced similar risks in nurturing a herd of dairy cows to produce quality milk.

Building a farm, raising a family, constructing a "big, beautiful brick house," and passing those achievements on to an appropriate family heir required intelligent planning and, sometimes, shrewd bargaining. Like residents of other German-American Catholic agrarian communities in Stearns County, the farmers of St. John the Baptist parish were unable to purchase and benefit from newly invented agricultural tools when they began to be available in the 1870s. National economic depression, locust plagues, and subsistence-level income certainly contributed to this slow movement toward mechanization. It was not until the 1890s that Meire Grove farmers mechanized their operations. By that time—having become convinced that wheat farming was too chancy an enterprise on which to depend—they were solidly committed to dairy farming, a reliable kind of agriculture traditionally practiced in the German-speaking lands from which they had come.

There is some wisdom in the conservative and secure path taken by these farm families. Because the power of the Church became incorporated into the workplaces of parishioners, they may have immediately and naturally relied on the sacraments and sacramentals as sources of spiritual rather than mechanical power to take their labors from year to year successfully. They saw the annual cycle of worship services, special holy days, and individual and family prayers as sufficient means by which to obtain both earthly and eternal security. Through these means, they believed, they were in touch with a divine power that would be sufficient to help them contend with the difficulties and occasional calamities of farming. In fact, once their operations had proven to be successful during the 1880s and 1890s, they could entertain the idea that they might indeed be God's chosen people. When they prayed, "Zu uns komme dein Reiche" (To us comes your Kingdom/Thy Kingdom come) from the Our Father, some parishioners may have believed that that Kingdom had already arrived. The fertile earth as blessed by the church gave them well-being and substance; the consecrated earth of the cemetery would provide the place for their last complete rest from labors before the day of new life dawned. But for now, a big, beautiful brick house, situated on a stable and successful farm, meant satisfaction and security.

VII

Election Day, Meire Grove, 1900

VII. COMPARISONS, CONCLUSIONS, AND A METAPHOR

As traced in this study, the history of St. John the Baptist parish during its formative years has provided a temporal framework within which to measure the physical growth of the community and describe the development of dairying as the basis of its stable economy. Exploration of the built environment created in this period has offered a means of grasping the importance of the parish's distinctive structures—particularly its numerous brick farmhouses, made of locally produced brick and constructed by skilled local masons and carpenters. Analysis of those substantial dwellings reveals that while they may have externally resembled American houses, the design and function of their interior spaces were traditionally German. Examination of the aesthetic qualities of these houses has shown that their form and decorative finish derived from a German-vernacular preference for simplicity, stability, and permanence. Additional perspective on the meaning of these houses has been offered through a look at their spiritual dimension, that is, their role as the homes of pious Catholics who participated fully in the religious life of the community.

From the beginning, St. John the Baptist parish was a German-American enclave, insulated from direct pressures to adapt to the dominant culture; it had been established under the nurturing auspices of the Church of Rome and was surrounded by Catholic parishes of similar ethnic composition. The immigrants built their community and patterned their lives according to the immediate physical challenges and opportunities of the new environment while also striving, whenever and wherever possible, to sustain the traditions of their Niedersachsen village culture. Though they certainly considered themselves to be Americans and proudly displayed the

Stars and Stripes at civic and religious celebrations alike, they became citizens according to their own timetable and on their own terms.

Supported by their religious faith and fortified by their tenacious hold on village culture, parishioners also actively maintained their native tongue in America—into the fourth generation. The rigorous and explicit structure of the German language reinforced patterns of thought and behavior that consistently reflected a conservative disposition toward change.

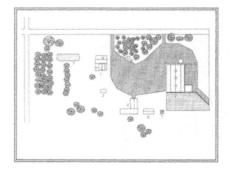

Like other farmers in the Upper Midwest, parishioners initially sought income through the cultivation of cash-grain crops; but atypically, they later chose dairying instead of diversified crop-and-livestock production or other specialized forms of agriculture. They were not entrepreneurs who sought to enlarge landholdings and profits. Rather, they worked with the purpose of caring for and maintaining relatively small, productive farms that would stay in the family. In some instances, a family realized a secure income on as little as eighty acres. These farmers would have agreed with another German-American, the late-twentieth-century economist Ernst Friedrich Schumacher, that "small is beautiful."[1]

As part of concluding this study, it will be instructive to examine the salient qualities of the parish and its inhabitants in relation to the national culture. Filling in this perspective will further enhance the reader's understanding of the ways the community was distinct while also illuminating characteristics it shared with the larger society of which it was a part. Three angles of view are relevant in establishing this perspective: a comparison of nineteenth-century models for domestic architecture and home life as prescribed by architectural-stylebook authors and social reformers with vernacular norms in the parish; an examination of national ideals about rural life and republican virtue as expressed by Thomas Jefferson and Ralph Waldo Emerson; and a comparison of the vision of national destiny and true citizenship as promulgated by Anglo-American historians with the process of becoming American as parishioners actually experienced it.

The building up of "big, beautiful brick houses" was a direct reflection of the essential beliefs and values shared by all members of St. John the Baptist parish. Detailed comparison of these houses with fashionable American house types indicates that parish dwellings differed considerably from the generally popular models.

An American ideal of cultured domesticity was first championed by Andrew Jackson Downing in the late 1840s and promoted by other architectural-stylebook authors through the 1870s. Believing that domestic architecture was a vital indicator of the nation's level of culture and standard of morality, Downing and others urged prospective homeowners to consider the designs their publications offered. They prescribed dwellings enlivened with revival-style ornament that, they believed, reflected a taste for picturesque beauty. While allowing for variations of scale and wherewithal, the stylebooks specified that the ideal American house should display interesting asymmetries of plan and elevation, bold variations of surface texture, and striking contrasts of light and shadow created by exterior decorative features. Ideally, too, the house was to be situated in a sylvan environment that was as picturesque as the structure itself.

In their 1869 book, *The American Woman's Home,* Catharine Beecher and Harriet Beecher Stowe (the reform-minded daughters of the Calvinist preacher Lyman Beecher) offered further advice on how to achieve a proper family atmosphere. Their program was considered "progressive" insofar as its "domestic economy" set forth what many saw as the best ways to maintain healthy conditions in the home, efficient methods to prepare and serve meals, and prudent tactics for budgeting household money. Like the stylebook authors, Beecher and Stowe illustrated their volume with practical floor plans for a house centered around a soundly functioning kitchen, equipped with the latest culinary conveniences.

These reform movements to shape the nature of domestic America were paralleled and strengthened by a series of revivals that swept through Protestant denominations from the 1840s to the 1860s. Sharing similar goals for the rearing of children in a religious environment, preachers, social reformers, and stylebook authors alike favored the Gothic-style house as quintessentially Christian—replete with a cross atop a central gable and end gables as appropriate ornamentation, stained-glass windows, and a parlor pump organ as features conducive to the creation of a pious atmosphere. Plans for such ideal houses offered a range of room sizes and prescribed functions to meet the various needs of the Christian family. A Beecher and Stowe-design kitchen served a family in which the father had a study stocked with edifying reading, the mother had a sewing room in which to pursue feminine crafts, and parents and children occupied separate, private bedchambers. Guests were greeted in the front entry hall, then all retired to the parlor where they would observe proper Victorian forms of socializing.[2]

Stylebook authors and social reformers such as Beecher and Stowe addressed their messages to an urban middle-class audience, to landed gentry who built country villas, and to progressive agrarians who lived in manorial farmhouses. Books such as Downing's and Beecher and Stowe's, magazines, local newspapers, and agricultural journals carried columns and illustrated features that spread the domestic-environment gospel to rural America. In St. John the Baptist parish, however, the language barrier kept these views from reaching many residents. While they learned enough English to transact business with the larger economic world, they used German in their local, everyday lives. Yet if parishioners had directly encountered these progressive Anglo-American ideas about house design and function, they would have considered them alien. For in setting up their farmhouses, they were guided by the deeply imbued values and customs they had inherited from the homeland. German-American families, like virtually all new citizens, dearly valued their homes. Indeed, the popular proverb "There's no place like home" is of German origin (*Eigener Herd ist Goldes wert*) but used universally to express a common sentiment.

On a practical level, parish families perceived the house as one work site among others on the farm, a place to perform essential tasks. The *Wohnküche/Flurküche* (all-purpose kitchen/entrance kitchen) qualities of the German-American kitchen helped foster social values of family cooperation, not to mention an open hospitality. On an aesthetic level, parishioners saw their brick farmhouses as manifestations of the security and durability they labored to achieve. And on a religious level, they believed their homes and

farm enterprises to be directly blessed through sacramental rituals that the parish priest performed on site. Their piety was devoid of the sentiment and emotional fervor that Anglo-American revivalists fostered; it was practical and immediate, grounded in the authority of the Church, and seen as efficacious because it had worked for their ancestors for centuries. Believing firmly that these old ways were the best ways, they saw no reason to adopt new forms of religious expression. Further, the local priest and the bishop of the diocese strove to protect parishioners from the non-Catholic influences of the surrounding world, both religious and secular.

Parishioners' remarkable ability to maintain their inherited identity in the challenging New World setting is epitomized by the great many parish-farmhouse floor plans—in brick and wooden dwellings alike—that employed the traditional Niedersachsen spatial template. Interior spaces were patterned to re-create the *Flurküche*, *Wohnzimmer*, and *Schlafkammern*, providing the family with ancestrally familiar chambers whose very forms profoundly reinforced their domestic, social, and religious values. In this way, the brick house that provided secure shelter also served as a spiritually nourishing place. A reversal of a biblical adage expresses the way parishioners' qualities of adaptability were reflected in their houses: *Sie füllten in neue Flaschen alte Wein.* (They filled new bottles with old wine.) They preserved their vintage domestic traditions in containers of recognizable American house types that they judged would be adequate for their needs.

Differences between St. John the Baptist parish and the dominant culture are also illuminated by contrasting the nature of parish farmers with the idealized qualities of the American agrarian, as outlined by several key thinkers. In his writings, Thomas Jefferson envisioned farmers as a stable, loyal population who would establish a social order in the new nation's expanding territories by creating family farms on relatively small tracts of land. As freeholders, these citizens of rural America would be independent, would freely speak their minds, and would vote their consciences as they participated in the governance of their own communities and the country as a whole.[3] "Cultivators of the earth are the most valuable citizens," he wrote to John Jay in 1785. "They are the most vigorous, the most independent, the most virtuous, and they are tied to their country and wedded to its liberty and interests by the most lasting bonds."[4] Jefferson's definition of the farmer's virtues was set squarely within an Enlightenment-based framework of ethics and civic duty.

American Romantic authors of the nineteenth century, particularly Ralph Waldo Emerson, enlarged the contours and intensified the colors of the virtuous yeoman's image. He extolled the farmer as a person who "stands close to Nature" and therefore "nearest to God, the first cause."[5] In Emerson's view, the agrarian's labors were fundamental because he obtained sustenance from the earth not only for himself but also others. The philosopher described the farmer physically as "deep-chested, long-winded, tough, slow and sure, and timely."[6] The farmer was also healthy: "We see [him] with pleasure and respect when we think what powers and utilities are so meekly worn."[7] Living in the presence of Nature, the farmer had an uncorrupted behavior that, in its innocence, offered an ideal of character and life. Emerson saw the yeoman as specially equipped to commune with Nature and God, both of which, in his transcendentalist view, were one and the same.

Jefferson as an Enlightenment thinker and Emerson as a Romantic pantheist obviously did not conceive of the ideal yeoman in terms of traditional Western Christianity, especially Roman Catholicism.[8] The agrarian perspective that informed the cautious, conservative style of dairy farming in St. John the Baptist parish originated in Church theology and was strengthened by beliefs and customs of peasant culture. Catholic teachings on agriculture first developed during the early Middle Ages and were based mainly on the writings of St. Augustine. These teachings characterized the farmer as a "lowly toiler" who was warned of the evils of this world and allured by the blessings of a heavenly destiny. Clergymen admonished the farmer not to accrue material treasures here in the City of Man but to store up spiritual riches that would be enjoyed in the City of God. Rather than strive for surplus and wealth, the pious farmer should simply seek reliable productivity and sufficiency. Thomas Aquinas further defined the pious peasant farmer as requiring discipline in order to perform faithfully his duties to his feudal lord and to the Lord of the Church.[9]

Admittedly, the farmers of St. John the Baptist parish did not ponder these abstractions as they walked to the barn to milk the cows or clean manure from their stalls. But while the link between theology and action was not direct, the teachings of the Church and the traditions of peasant culture did provide a structure within which the theological conceptions of farm labor could be realized. Given this, it is ironic that German-American farmers embodied the ideals of Jefferson's virtuous yeoman more fully than did the kind of American farmer who exploited the land for large profits. Certainly, farmers in the parish were freeholders who were fiercely loyal to their land. They were a stable, responsible element of the new nation's society. And, to satisfy Emerson's ideal, they were religious. However, they practiced these virtues within the context of their own Catholic faith and folk heritage. Their pride in the value of their work was epitomized in the old German motto *Ackerwerk—Wacherwerk.* (Farm work is valiant work.)

During the decades when settlers in the developing parish were obtaining federal lands and becoming nationalized, American scholars were interpreting the meaning of the frontier experience and the larger destiny of the United States. By 1900, the prophecy Father Franz Pierz had made in 1855 that Germans would prove themselves to be "the most proficient farmers and the best Catholics" seemed fulfilled. Scholars typically failed, however, to recognize these immigrants as belonging to the chosen people who would to inherit the Promised Land.[10] The historian Charles Beard, for example, defined qualities of an ideal American according to values of the dominant culture. Assuming a generally shared belief in progress, Beard and his contemporaries looked to reason and science to effect positive change in America. In order to pursue this path to the nation's future alongside their new fellow citizens, the immigrants would need to shed their Old World ways. Thus the very beliefs and values that shaped the life of St. John the Baptist parish were seen as retrograde and counterproductive. Blinded by their beatific vision of American destiny, historians adhering to this position failed to perceive the rich cultural diversity that was, and remains, basic to this country's health and strength.[11] Unaware of interpretations of national history that prescribe traits of true American citizenship, St. John the Baptist parish and many ethnic neighborhoods and communities have consistently and quietly contributed to the building of the nation and to the well-being of its democratic order.

The hundreds of thousands of bricks that composed the walls of the Church of St. John the Baptist, of the village stores, and of parish farmhouses can be perceived as a metaphor for the way of life in this German-American enclave. The brickmason laid up his materials in fixed patterns that gave the walls strength and cohesion. Similarly, family members worked together, performing household and farmyard chores in time-honored patterns. They milked the cows twice a day and carefully followed established methods of processing the milk. They periodically cleaned the stalls and the barn. Two or three times each summer, they harvested hay by pitching up fork after fork from field to wagon and from wagon to loft. They repeated these tasks every year of their lives in a consistent, thorough way. Just as the labors of the farm structured time, the sacraments of the Church clearly marked out parishioners' lives as they grew to adulthood and fulfilled their devotional duties. The clergy organized the relationships of individuals, families, and groups within the congregation. The liturgical calendar ordered time through the celebration of ritual sacramentals.

The predictable rhythmic pattern of enduring bricks, the continual rounds of farm chores, and the ordained cycle of times to receive the sacraments and celebrate sacramentals were essentials of being a German-American Roman Catholic in St. John the Baptist parish. The experience of life for a parishioner "as an integral, steadfast, component of the system" was immediate and direct.[12] Worship and work performed in an environment built by their own hands became a single design within which the members of this community preserved their faith, practiced their values, and perpetuated their culture.

NOTES

NOTES TO CHAPTER 1

1. The spelling *Meyer's Grove* was given in a published history of the village. See Paulin Blecker, *Deep Roots: One Hundred Years of Catholic Life in Meire Grove* (St. Cloud, Minn.: Sentinel Publishing, 1958), 103. Despite the *Meire's Grove* spelling variation that appears in the 1896 and 1925 plats of Grove Township, the name *Meire Grove* was given in the U.S. Census of 1905. The family name Meyer appears as early as the ninth century as Meyer von Holdorpe and Meire von Holdorpe in land records for the village of Holdorf, Oldenburg. A few families in St. John the Baptist parish can trace their lineage back to the time of Charlemagne. Other local surnames, such as Gramke, Klaphake, and Schulte, appear in Holdorf village records of the fifteenth and sixteenth centuries. See Gemeinde Holdorf, *Gemeindechronik Holdorf, 1188–1988* [History of the Village of Holdorf, 1188–1988] (Vechta, West Germany: Vechtaer Druckerei und Verlag, 1988), 55–61, 150–64.

2. Contributors to the recently published scholarly anthology *Migration, Migration History, History* discuss basic reasons for the migration of individuals and groups from their homelands. Regarding migration as a "normal and structural element of human society throughout history," the editors note that the most basic individual motivations are choice of occupation and/or life partner. The great migration in which parishioners of St. John the Baptist were involved occurred during a period when people throughout Europe chose to leave their native lands for what appeared to be greater economic opportunities in other parts of the world, especially America. See Jan Lucassen and Leo Lucassen, eds., *Migration, Migration History, History: Old Paradigms and New Perspectives* (Bern: Peter Lang, 1997), 9–38.

3. Hildegard Binder Johnson, "Factors Influencing the Distribution of the German Pioneer Population in Minnesota," *Agricultural History* 19 (January 1945): 55.

4. Ibid., quoting "Eine kurze Beschreibung des Minnesota Territoriums" [A Brief Writing about the Minnesota Territory], published as an appendix to *Die Indianer in Nord-Amerika, Gebräuche, u.s.w.* [The Indians of North America, Customs, etc.](St. Louis, 1855).

5. Sister Mary Gilbert Kelly, "The Work of Bishop Loras and Father Pierz for Colonization," *Catholic Immigrant Colonization Projects in the United States, 1815–60*, United States Catholic Historical Society Series, no. 17 (New York: United States Catholic Historical Society, 1939), 166, 167.

6. Inholf Voegler, "The Roman Catholic Culture Region of Western Minnesota," *Pioneer America* 8, no. 2 (1976): 74, 77. The Benedictine Fathers and Sisters alike came from German-settlement areas in Pennsylvania.

7. William Bell Mitchell, *The History of Stearns County, Minnesota* (Chicago: H. C. Cooper, Jr., 1915), 1:198–99.

8. Johnson, "Factors Influencing": 55.

9. Ibid.: 56. See also Kathleen Neils Conzen, *Making Their Own America: Assimilation Theory and the German Peasant Pioneer* (New York: Berg, 1990), 18–19.

10. Mitchell, *History of Stearns County*, 2:1020–21.

11. Payment for the land that the Meire Grove pioneers preempted was not due until late 1860, allowing them more than two years to break the soil, plant and harvest crops, build shelters, and save up payment money. See Conzen, *Making Their Own America*, 17. The Homestead Act that passed Congress in 1862 offered 160 acres of land to any adult head of household, male or female, who was (or was in the process of becoming) a United States citizen. The claimant paid a $10 registration fee, lived on and improved the land for five years, and paid a "proving up" or $5 filing fee to secure full title.

12. Blecker, *Deep Roots*, 23.

13. Marilyn Brinkman et al., *Bringing Home the Cows: Family Dairy Farming in Stearns County, 1853–1986* (St. Cloud, Minn.: Stearns County Historical Society, 1988), 8–12.

14. Fred A. Shannon, *The Farmer's Last Frontier: Agriculture, 1860–1897*, vol. 5 of *The Economic History of the United States* (New York: Holt, Rinehart and Winston, 1963), 417.

15. Ibid., 416.

16. German peasant proverbs are imbued with centuries of experience and practical wisdom. Many of them couch a combined message and lesson in positive terms. Others contain images and words that graphically portray the harsher aspects of farm life. See Ernst Böhm, "Aberglaube und Sagen aus der Gemeinde Holdorf" [Superstitions and Legends of the Holdorf Community], in *Gemeindechronik Holdorf*, 689–95; and Anneliese Müller-Hegermann and Luise Otto, *Das Kleine Sprichtwort-Buch* [The Small Book of Proverbs] (Leipzig: Ver Bibliographisches Institut, 1965).

17. Blecker, *Deep Roots*, 39–40.

18. Roger R. Imdieke, "Herman G. Imdieke Biography" (manuscript, St. Cloud, Minn.: Stearns County Historical Society, n.d.), 6.

19. The mechanical cream separator was invented in Scandinavia in 1878 and first appeared in the United States in 1879. See John T. Schlebecker, *A History of American Dairying* (Chicago: Rand McNally, 1967), 26. By 1885 an affordable hand-powered separator became available for use on farms.

20. In 1898 W. A. John Henry published the first edition of *Feeds and Feeding*, which provided basic information about the bovine diet that would result in the best milk production. See Schlebecker, *American Dairying*, 39.

21. Ibid., 31–34.

22. Mitchell, *History of Stearns County*, 2:1023.

23. Brinkman, *Bringing Home the Cows*, 16–18.

24. One force inspiring the creation of a cooperative creamery in Meire Grove was near at hand. Theophilus Haecker, popularly known as the Father of Cooperatives and the Father of Dairying in Minnesota, started the School of Dairying at the University of Minnesota's College of Agriculture in 1891. By 1898 there were 560 cooperatives operating in Minnesota, established largely as a result of his statewide travels to explain the benefits of such organizations. Brinkman, *Bringing Home the Cows*, 27.

25. Blecker, *Deep Roots*, 62. In 1986 Stearns County led all other Minnesota counties in the production of dairy products and was among the top ten dairy-producing counties in the nation. Brinkman, *Bringing Home the Cows*, 5.

26. For studies noting the key role played by the ethnic church in maintaining German-American separateness, see Kathleen Neils Conzen, "Historical Approaches to the Study of Rural Ethnic Communities," in Frederick C. Luebke, ed., *Ethnicity on the Great Plains* (Lincoln: University of Nebraska Press, 1980), 1–18; and David Peterson, "'From Bone Depth': German-American Communities in Rural Minnesota before the Great War," *Journal of American Ethnic History* 11 (winter 1992): 27–55.

27. Census data do not support the custom in Stearns County of identifying parishes with a single place of origin in German-speaking lands. Of the 115 people listed in the 1880 Grove Township census, 52 cited Prussia as their place of birth, 11 named Bavaria, 17 reported that they were from Oldenburg, and a few apiece claimed to have come from Austria, Bohemia, Hanover, Hesse Darmstad, Luxembourg, and Saxony. See United States manuscript population census schedules, 1880, for Grove Township, Stearns County, Minnesota (microfilm, St. Paul: Minnesota Historical Society).

28. Blecker, *Deep Roots*, 84, 86.

29. C. Brauns, *Praktische Belehrungen und Rathschläge für Reisende und Auswanderer nach Amerika* [Practical Instructions and Advice for Travelers and Emigrants to America] (Braunschweig: Waisenhaus Buchdruckerei, 1829), frontispiece page.

30. In fact, the German language was used for instruction in many rural Stearns County schools until just after World War II, when consolidation closed most of the one-room schoolhouses that were still strongly influenced by the parish in which the given school was located. See Conzen, *Making Their Own America*, 29. From 1830 to the 1860s anxieties generated by major social and economic changes brought about by industrialization, urbanization, and mass immigration led many Americans to turn upon certain foreign groups and Catholics as scapegoats. Members of the Know-Nothing Party, which had its greatest strength in the

1850s, believed that immigrants should become "Americanized" by learning and using English. Further, they asserted that immigrants should assimilate American ways of life and not live clannishly together. This nativist party singled out the urban Irish Catholics for vicious and violent attacks. German Catholics were also their targets; but because German Catholics were the dominant majority in Stearns County, they did not directly experience nativist pressures. The clerical colonizers' efforts to establish solid ethnic-religious enclaves were in part intended to protect settlers in the Diocese of St. Cloud from possible persecution. See Ira M. Leonard and Robert D. Parmet, *American Nativism, 1830–1860* (New York: Van Norstrand, 1971).

31. See E. Z. Vogt, Jr., "Social Stratification in the Rural Midwest: A Structural Analysis," *Rural Sociology* 12 (1947): 364–75.

32. Blecker, *Deep Roots*, 61.

33. For a discussion illuminating social life in another rural setting, see Jane Marie Pederson, "The Country Visitor: Patterns of Hospitality in Rural Wisconsin, 1880–1925," *Agricultural History* 58 (July 1984): 347–64.

34. Ronald G. Klietsch, "The Religious Social System of the German Catholics of the Sauk" (master's thesis, University of Minnesota, 1958), 182–87.

35. Takenori Inoki, *Aspects of German Peasant Emigration to the United States, 1815–1914: A Reexamination of Some Behavioral Hypotheses in Migration Theory* (New York: Arno Press, 1981), 113–14.

36. Investigation of land records for Grove, Getty, Spring Hill, and Lake George Townships in the 1850s indicates that all parcels of land were originally claimed, through the preemption process, at the set price of $1.25 an acre. Because many of the area's first settlers arrived with little or no money, they were unable to pay for their parcels immediately. After 1862 many filed homestead claims for land already "held" by preemption. One means of acquiring the land succeeded the other, and both means were employed in turn in order to demonstrate legal title.

37. Plats for Getty, Grove, Lake George, and Spring Hill Townships from 1896 to 1947 identify land held by St. John the Baptist parishioners. The maps record a remarkably high rate of tenure, with the same family names remaining attached to tracts varying in size from 40 to 250 acres.

38. There were not enough acres of farmland in the townships to enable every son born in the parish to inherit, or negotiate ownership of the family farm from his father. Families helped sons and married daughters who did not remain in the parish get started on farms elsewhere in the state. Also, around 1900, some young people left the parish to homestead land in North Dakota; and by about 1920, another group departed for Alberta, Canada, when homestead land became available in that province. Lena Mueller, interview by author, Lake Henry, Minn., July 17, 1997.

39. See Conzen, *Making Their Own America*, 21–25.

40. Mack Walker, *Germany and the Emigration, 1816–1885* (Cambridge, Mass.: Harvard University Press, 1964), 69.

41. Blecker, *Deep Roots*, 89–90.

42. Herbert Krause, *The Thresher* (Indianapolis, Ind.: Bobbs-Merrill, 1946), 125–26.

NOTES TO CHAPTER II

1. Accounts of the settlers' first habitations differ. One source claims that Henry Meyer constructed a log cabin soon after arriving in Stearns County in June 1858. See Paulin Blecker, *Deep Roots: One Hundred Years of Catholic Life in Meire Grove* (St. Cloud, Minn.: Sentinel Publishing, 1958), 21. It seems unlikely, however, that he and his brother, Herman, would have had enough time to cut down the trees, prepare the logs, and construct the shelter before the onset of winter. In an interview, Dale Imdieke talked about the Meyer dugout shelter. He pointed out a small depression in a hillside on the Meyer farm where, he claimed, the dugout had been located. Dale Imdieke, interview by author, Meire Grove, Minn., October 11, 1983.

2. For an account of dugout construction on the Dakota frontier, see Gustav O. Sandro, *The Immigrants' Trek: A Detailed History of the Lake Hendricks Colony in Brookings County, Dakota Territory, 1873–1881* (Hendricks, Minn.: Author, 1929), 19–23. Another firsthand account explains: "There was the dug-out usually in a side-hill, with a sod roof, a few studdings

and boards being used to support the roof. The walls and the floor were usually native earth." John B. Reese, *Some Pioneers and Pilgrims on the Prairies of Dakota* (Mitchell, S.Dak.: Author, 1920), 38.

3. Blecker, *Deep Roots,* 21.

4. See Terry G. Jordan, *American Log Buildings: An Old World Heritage* (Chapel Hill: University of North Carolina Press, 1985), 26–28.

5. Blecker, *Deep Roots,* 21; and William Bell Mitchell, *The History of Stearns County, Minnesota* (Chicago: H. C. Cooper, Jr., 1915), 2:1020–21.

6. For a discussion of log cabins in Stearns County, see Marilyn Salzi Brinkman and William Towner Morgan, *Light from the Hearth: Central Minnesota Pioneers and Early Architecture* (St. Cloud, Minn.: North Star Press, 1982), 26–48.

7. The house represented in figs. 2:4a and 2:4b no longer stands. The floor plans and elevations here are reconstructions based on the photograph and on an interview with a woman who was born and raised in the house. Marcia Klaphake, interview by author, Meire Grove, Minn., April 27, 1996.

8. The names for the various spaces in these early houses are here given in the German to indicate their ethnic origin, their specific or general function, and the words parishioners used to identify them. *Wohnküche,* for instance, connotes an all-purpose chamber used not only as a kitchen but also for many other domestic purposes.

9. Blecker, *Deep Roots,* 26.

10. Ibid.

11. See Fred B. Kniffen and Henry Glassie, "Building in Wood in the Eastern United States: A Time-Place Perspective," *Geographical Review* 56 (1966): 48–51. Examples of Stearns County vertical-log constructions by German and Slovenian pioneers are discussed in Brinkman and Morgan, *Light from the Hearth,* 59–61.

12. See Gemeinde Holdorf, *Gemeindechronik Holdorf, 1188–1988* [History of the Village of Holdorf, 1188–1988] (Vechta, West Germany: Vechtaer Druckerei und Verlag, 1988), 55–61; and Hermann Kaiser and Helmut Ottenjann, "Zur Geschichte des niederdeutschen Hallenhauses [Toward a History of the Northern German Hallenhaus (House-Barn)]," *Museumsdorf Cloppenburg: Niedersächsisches Freilichtmuseum* [Cloppenburg Village Museum: Niedersachsen Open Air Museum](Cloppenburg, West Germany: Niedersächsisches Freilichtmuseum Verlag, 1988), 109–15.

13. Blecker, *Deep Roots,* 37–38.

14. For instance, a biographical sketch of Michael Theisen, who taught at Meire Grove for nine years, notes that he attended district schools near Cold Spring, Minnesota, was a student at the Pontifical Collegium Yosephinum in Columbus, Ohio, and spent three years at St. John's College in Collegeville, Minnesota. See Mitchell, *History of Stearns County,* 2:1020.

15. This blend of secular and sacred education was not unusual in rural school districts where one ethnic group sharing the same religious faith established and operated the township school as a church or parish school. See Fred W. Peterson, *Homes in the Heartland: Balloon Frame Farmhouses of the Upper Midwest, 1850–1920* (Lawrence: University Press of Kansas, 1992), 161–68; and Andrew Gulliford, *America's Country Schools* (Washington, D.C.: Preservation Press, 1984).

16. The 1870 U.S. Census lists two German-American carpenters in Grove Township, John Santhe and J. H. Weisherman, who were probably involved in the building of the frame church. Both were then old enough (thirty-one and forty-five, respectively) to have had sufficient building experience. See United States manuscript population census schedule, 1870, for Grove Township, Stearns County, Minnesota (microfilm, St. Paul: Minnesota Historical Society).

17. One account describes the church as measuring 80 by 30 feet. See Mitchell, *History of Stearns County,* 1:229–30. Analysis of a photograph of the structure, however, indicates that its dimensions were approximately as given in the present text.

18. The floor plan of the second Church of St. John the Baptist shown here (fig. 2:7b) is a reconstruction based on the photograph of the church (fig. 2:7a), which was analyzed for measurement, proportions, and construction as well on the basis of the author's knowledge of timber-frame, braced-frame, and balloon-frame structures.

19. Fig. 2:9a shows the house as modified to function as a granary. The windows have been made smaller, and the chimney has been removed.

20. This is the earliest documented appearance in the parish of the *Pfostenwohnhaus* spatial template. It was repeatedly used, with variations, during the 1880s and as late as 1915 in parish farmhouses made of brick. The perpetuation of this model over several generations is yet another example of how deeply rooted various vernacular traditions were in the consciousness of these German-Americans.

21. These are the dimensions given in Blecker, *Deep Roots*, 46. In its story on the dedication of the church, the *St. Cloud Journal Press* reported that the building cost $30,000, that it was 64 feet wide and 152 feet long, and that it had a spire rising 162 feet. *St. Cloud (Minn.) Journal Press*, July 22, 1886, 3.

22. For a description of the cost and complexity involved in building a comparable church in Stearns County, see *Centennial 1881–1981, "Heritage of Faith," Sacred Heart Parish, Freeport, Minnesota* (Chicago: C. P. D. Corporation, 1981), unpaginated.

23. *Der Nordstern* (St. Cloud, Minn.), October 1, 1884, 8.

24. *St. Cloud (Minn.) Journal Press*, March 21, 1872, 4.

25. John Herman Kropp, Biographical File, Heritage Center, Stearns County Historical Society, St. Cloud, Minn. A dating of structures on the basis of fieldwork indicates that the church was the first large mortise-and-tenon timber-frame structure in the parish. About a decade later, parish farmer-builders and carpenters began erecting large dairy barns, evidently drawing upon the knowledge and skill they had gained in constructing the church. When completed in about 1900, the gambrel-roofed Henry Imdieke dairy barn, located across Church Street from the sanctuary, rose to the same height as the central ridge of the church roof.

26. Mitchell, *History of Stearns County*, 1:659–60. Mitchell's account of Lethert's work includes mention of the carpenter's Germanic love of beer. Despite the dangers involved, he insisted that, before he ascended the scaffolding to labor on the steeple frame, a bucket of beer (about ninety-six ounces) be hoisted in place to see him through the dry parts of the day.

27. Blecker, *Deep Roots*, 62–63.

28. Mitchell interprets the context of religious faith in which the Church of St. John the Baptist and others nearby came into being: "The development of Catholicity in Stearns County is a monument to the deep faith and loyalty of the people who made these achievements possible. In the midst of their poverty they found the means to raise proud church edifices and schools; many of them donated parcels of land for the church or for the cemetery, and others contributed to the furnishing and embellishment of their church with altars, pulpit, statuary, organ, bells, or vestments. Did they feel a loss? Look at their contented faces, at their comfortable homes, their broad fields. Like the other children of men, they go about their temporal pursuits six days of the week, but when Sunday comes, they all assemble in the great house they fondly call 'our church,' which their fathers or themselves had built." Mitchell, *History of Stearns County*, 1:199.

29. See Charles Sholl, *Working Designs for Ten Catholic Churches, Containing All Dimensions, Details, and Specifications* (New York: D. and J. Sadler, 1869); and George Bowler, *Chapel and Church Architecture with Designs for Parsonages* (Boston: J. P. Jewett, 1856). The architectural historian Phoebe Stanton claims that "the small, rural Roman Catholic country church, which was something of a rarity in the United States, was most often [a] responsibility of the local priest and his flock." See Phoebe Stanton, *The Gothic Revival and American Church Architecture: An Episode in Taste, 1840–1856* (Baltimore, Md.: Johns Hopkins University Press, 1968), 248–49.

30. The parish church in Holdorf, Oldenburg, built in 1827, was of a neo-Gothic style both inside and out. The parish church in nearby Damme was also neo-Gothic and had a richly appointed interior similar to that of the Church of St. John the Baptist in Meire Grove. See Ulrich Stille, *Dome, Kirchen, und Kloster in Niedersachsen* [Cathedrals, Churches, and Cloisters in Niedersachsen] (Frankfurt am Main, West Germany: W. Weidlich, 1963).

31. The structure was rebuilt, almost immediately, on the foundation of the 1885 church; it stands today. At that time, people living in the southern portion of the parish

formed a separate congregation and built a church at Greenwald, just four miles south of Meire Grove. The fact that the Soo Line railroad had developed Greenwald could have been a factor distinguishing people living there from inhabitants of the Meire Grove area. Nonetheless, it is ironic that this division occurred at a time when automobile transportation made travel easier and faster. Blecker, *Deep Roots,* 86–88.

32. As in other exclusively Catholic enclaves in the Diocese of St. Cloud, residence in St. John the Baptist parish automatically meant membership in the church. Thus all increase was manifested in one congregation. This kind of structural expansion, which directly reflected the population growth of a single religious group, was relatively rare in the rural Upper Midwest. In the late nineteenth and early twentieth centuries, most rural areas had heterogeneous populations, and many churches served a variety of faiths.

33. Henry Letner, "'Home . . .': What It Means to a Minnesota Junior Dairyman," *The Kraftsman* 2 (summer 1953): unpaginated.

34. One farmhouse made of Imdieke brick had been completed and another was under way by the time the church was built. A comparison of the uneven quality of brick in the Henry Imdieke farmhouse (1883, fig. 4:11a) with the consistent quality of the brick in the Ferdinand Eveslage farmhouse (ca. 1885–86, fig. 4:4a) indicates that, by 1885, the Imdiekes had found the recipe they were seeking.

35. During all the years it operated, from about 1881 to 1915, the factory made only common bricks. Because of their relative lack of density and hardness, such bricks would not have been suitable for the outer walls of the grand edifice of the church; they lacked the finer appearance of finished brick. Dale Imdieke, interview by author, Meire Grove, Minn., October 23, 1995; and Blecker, *Deep Roots,* 61.

36. A handwritten inventory of village businesses was compiled for the parish's centennial celebration in 1958. See Al Vornbrock notebook, Meire Grove City File, Heritage Center, Stearns County Historical Society, St. Cloud, Minn.

37. See Robert E. Dickinson, *The Regions of Germany* (New York: Oxford University Press, 1945), 132–39; and

Anthony T. Rozycki, "The Evolution of the Hamlets of Stearns County, Minnesota" (master's thesis, University of Minnesota, 1977).

38. The village plans shown in figs. 2:19 and 2:22 are based on published plats and plans of Meire Grove and Holdorf, respectively; included are the locations and identifications of as many structures as I have been able to verify. See *Plat Book of Stearns County, Minnesota, 1896* (Philadelphia: Pinkney and Brown, 1896); and *Gemeindechronik Holdorf,* 68–79, 134.

NOTES TO CHAPTER III

1. "Grove Homesteader Summoned by Death," *Melrose (Minn.) Beacon,* April 5, 1928, 1; and Roger R. Imdieke, "Herman G. Imdieke Biography" (manuscript, St. Cloud, Minn.: Stearns County Historical Society, n.d.), 5.

2. In Grove Township, a clay subsoil lay under the black-loam surface soil. Sand could be sifted from some light soils and could also be found along the banks of streams and the Sauk River. See William Bell Mitchell, *The History of Stearns County, Minnesota* (Chicago: H. C. Cooper, Jr., 1915), 2:1270.

3. One account claims that Herman Imdieke was encouraged to begin brick production to furnish material for the second Church of St. John the Baptist in Meire Grove, built in 1885 and dedicated in 1886. Paulin Blecker, *Deep Roots: One Hundred Years of Catholic Life in Meire Grove* (St. Cloud, Minn.: Sentinel Publishing, 1958), 44–46. Another version of the brickyard's origin is based on the recollections of Herman's grandson Fred Imdieke. This story has it that Herman thought of making brick while chinking his log cabin with straw and clay. With the help of his brother in Cincinnati he secured the equipment and began production in 1880. Henry Letner, "'Home . . .': What It Means to a Minnesota Junior Dairyman," *The Kraftsman* 2 (summer 1953): unpaginated. According to a third story, Herman and Joseph Imdieke, who had both worked in a brick-yard in Cincinnati, first tried making brick in Meire Grove in 1882 in order to satisfy German settlers' desire for brick houses. No quality product was made until

1885, after Herman had hired Ignatz Greve to formulate a proper recipe from local clay and sand. See Imdieke, "Herman G. Imdieke Biography."

4. The soft brick and the hard brittle brick may both have come from one firing of a kiln. As noted later in this chapter, bricks that are closest to the fire become extremely hard, while those on the outer perimeter of the kiln tend to fire to a softer material.

5. Letner, "'Home . . .,'" *The Kraftsman*.

6. Ibid.

7. Imdieke, "Herman G. Imdieke Biography," 5–6.

8. For descriptions of making brick, see Karl Gurcke, *Bricks and Brickmaking: A Handbook for Historical Archeology* (Moscow: University of Idaho Press, 1988), 338; and Harley J. McKee, *Introduction to Early American Masonry: Stone, Brick, Mortar, and Plaster* (New York: Columbia University Press, 1973), 41–59.

9. J. W. Crary, Sr., *Sixty Years a Brickmaker: A Practical Treatise on Brickmaking and Burning* (Indianapolis, Ind.: T. A. Randall, 1890), 8.

10. William A. Radford, *Radford's Brick Houses and How to Build Them* (Chicago: Radford Architectural Company, 1912), 10.

11. Crary, *Sixty Years a Brickmaker*, 18.

12. Some brickmakers used fired brick at the base and for the outer walls of the kiln in order to reduce this kind of loss of brick from the firing.

13. Gurcke, *Bricks and Brickmaking*, 35.

14. As Imdieke brick aged, it became somewhat redder but basically retained its distinctive red-orange color. The color was a product of the chemicals and minerals in the locally quarried clay and sand that composed the brick. Brick made in St. Martin Township, Stearns County, is pale yellow. Farther east in the county, one notes brick of a deep red hue. No history of Stearns County brick factories has been written; this information is drawn from the author's general survey fieldwork in the county.

15. Crary, *Sixty Years a Brickmaker*, 20. A cord is equal to 128 cubic feet of wood or a stack 8 feet long, 4 feet wide, and 4 feet high.

16. Brick kilns, lime furnaces, and iron-smelting operations were located near many villages and towns in the northwestern German provinces. Many in the parish were therefore already familiar with the spectacle of fire and fumes created by the firing of kilns.

17. Crary, *Sixty Years a Brickmaker*, 75.

18. Al Imdieke, interview by author, Valley City, N.Dak., September 22, 1988.

19. It seems that the bricklayer was the person chiefly responsible for the process of construction because the nature and pace of his work determined when the carpenters could set the joists at the foundation and the other elevations as well as build the roof and complete the interior of the house.

20. See Peter Rockwell, *The Art of Stoneworking: A Reference Guide* (Cambridge, England: Cambridge University Press, 1993), 18–19, 23–24.

21. Al Imdieke, interview.

22. For instance, the John and Catherine Schmiesing farmhouse (figs. 4:24a, 4:24b) originally was to be constructed according to a rectangular floor plan similar to that used in the Arnold Nietfeld farmhouse (fig. 4:19b). The joists delivered to the building site were long enough to overlap by about 12 to 14 inches at the center basement line. But Schmiesing died before construction began, and the house plan was modified to become a Foursquare. The joists set in the first floor overlap almost 36 inches. They were cut to order for the first plan and not cut for the modified plan. Builders seem to have been reluctant to waste time and energy recutting each joist.

23. See Steven Cleo Martens, "Ethnic Tradition and Innovation as Influences on a Rural, Midwestern Building Vernacular: Findings from Investigation of Brick Houses in Carver County, Minnesota" (master's thesis, University of Minnesota, 1988), 59, 77.

24. Bricklayers sometimes wet bricks before laying them in place because a dry brick absorbed too much moisture from the mortar and weakened the bond. In order to force mortar into irregularities of surface and pores on the brick, the bricklayer first spread the mortar on the last course of brick, lightly laid a brick on the mortar, and then shoved it diagonally across the mortar against the next brick. These steps were rhythmic movements instinctively performed by the experienced bricklayer. See Radford, *Radford's Brick Houses*, 25.

25. It was claimed that a good bricklayer could set up courses of brick without the aid of plumb lines. A master mason had experienced hands and a trained eye that served to gauge the trueness of a wall. Conrad Nietfeld, interview by author, Melrose, Minn., April 4, 1992.

26. A local supply of lime, a basic ingredient for mortar, came from the Illies farm in Grove Township, where August Illies operated a lime kiln with his working-age sons. One of his great-granddaughters recalled that he woke the boys at 2:00 A.M. in order to stoke the fires for a day's burning of material. Although there were no limestone rock deposits to quarry in the township, there was a considerable amount of limestone gravel deposited by glacial drift. Illies and his sons apparently burned or calcined this material. By the early 1870s, lime and mortar could be purchased at the Borgerding Lumber Yard in Melrose. Lena Mueller, interview by author, Lake Henry, Minn., July 17, 1997. See also Norman Davey, *A History of Building Materials* (London: Phoenix House, 1961), 97–111; and Mitchell, *History of Stearns County*, 1:3–10.

27. The efficiency experts of the Radford Architectural Company analyzed the labor of the bricklayer and arrived at the following average work-speed figures: 1,500 bricks could be laid in a ten-hour day if the joints remained rough; and 1,000 bricks could be laid if the joints were finished. See Radford, *Radford's Brick Houses*, 238.

28. See Chapter Five for a discussion of parishioners' aesthetic preferences with regard to local architecture.

29. See Fred W. Peterson, *Homes in the Heartland: Balloon Frame Farmhouses of the Upper Midwest, 1850–1920* (Lawrence: University Press of Kansas, 1992).

30. The fact that one-third of the houses in the parish were built of brick means that the parish had a higher-than-average number of such houses compared to other rural American neighborhoods. Approximately one-third of the frame houses were built from 1870 to 1885, before the brickyard was in operation. Another one-third of the frame houses were built after 1885, many of these after 1915, the year the brickyard closed. In a brief, informal biography of his father, Herman G. Imdieke (a son of the brick factory's cofounder), Roger

Imdieke wrote: "In retrospect, the demand for bricks was probably never that great. Some of the settlers believed that because they had brick houses in Germany, they needed brick houses and churches here. However, had nobody made bricks in the area, the churches would have bought the bricks somewhere else, and the houses built of bricks would have been built of logs." Imdieke, "Herman G. Imdieke Biography," 6.

31. This figure is based upon the recall of a daughter of the family, as conveyed by Dale Imdieke, letter to author, November 2, 1988.

32. Itemized wages: stonemason $80 for foundation, bricklayer @$3 a day for thirty days = $90; two carpenters @$1.50 a day for thirty days = $90; two laborers @$.75 a day for thirty days = $45. These estimates are based in part on local information and in part on the regional scale of wages for skilled and unskilled craftsmen in the period under discussion. Although presented as thirty-day estimates, they are not meant to imply that a house would be built in that time.

33. Carl Rheingans, the husband of a daughter of Gundar Lund, who built the house, claimed that the $2,800 figure is based upon receipts for the construction that are in the family's possession. Carl Rheingans, interview by author, Lac qui Parle County, Minn., September 4, 1984.

34. In 1912 the Radford Architectural Company published a book of plans for brick houses. It listed two models comparable in size to the Haverkamp farmhouse at prices considerably higher than the local vernacular brick structure. Radford model no. 9555 (40 x 37½ feet) listed between $9,725 and $10,025; plan no. 9538 (28½ by 39 feet) cost between $6,575 and $6,975. Radford, *Radford's Brick Houses*, 166, 158, 219.

NOTES TO CHAPTER IV

1. Henry Letner, "Home . . .': What It Means to a Minnesota Junior Dairyman," *The Kraftsman* 2 (summer 1953): unpaginated. According to various verbally rendered accounts, parish families built between fifty and sixty farmhouses in the area. These estimates are

not based on the material evidence that identifies houses that still exist or for which there is conclusive evidence of existence, such as photographs or surviving foundations of razed houses.

The present study is based on thirty-two brick farmhouses in the parish that either remain standing or for which there are photographic records. These houses, listed according to type, are:

Cross-Wing Type
Henry Berling, Section 6, Grove Township*
Jacob Botz, Section 9, Getty Township*
J. A. Caspers, Section 17, Grove Township*
Frank Deters, Section 2, Lake Shore Township
Ferdinand Eveslage, Section 4, Spring Hill Township
Henry Haverkamp, Section 24, Getty Township*
August Illies, Section 30, Grove Township
Henry Imdieke, Meire Grove village
Herman Imdieke, Section 4, Grove Township
George Kind, Section 20, Getty Township
Herman Quade, Section 17, Getty Township*
Herman Schmiesing, Section 24, Getty Township
Norman Wehlage, Section 24, Getty Township

Consolidated Rectangular-Mass Type
Ignatz Eibensteiner, Section 23, Getty Township
John Eibensteiner, Section 24, Getty Township
August Eveslage, Section 4, Spring Hill Township*
Joseph Imdieke, Section 7, Grove Township*
F. A. Meyer, Section 19, Grove Township
Henry Meyer, Section 18, Grove Township
Arnold Nietfeld, Section 4, Spring Hill Township
B. H. Otte, Section 5, Grove Township
J. B. Pallauch, Section 32, Melrose Township
Andrew Thull, Section 32, Grove Township
Mathias Winter, Section 32, Grove Township

Consolidated Square-Mass Type
Richard Imdieke, Section 15, Grove Township*
August Klaphake, Section 5, Grove Township
J. B. Schmiesing, Section 24, Grove Township
John Schmiesing, Section 13, Getty Township*
C. Van Beck, Section 6, Spring Hill Township*
Al Vornbrock, Section 23, Getty Township
(Two Foursquare houses in Meire Grove village)

* Houses bearing stone name-and-date inscription panels on their principal facades.

It is difficult to reach a consensus on the nature and nomenclature of folk and vernacular house types in the United States because there exist so many regional adaptations of types and local names for a bewildering variety of structures. Virtually every attempt to assert a definitive typology creates controversy. The classification of house types into two simple groups here applies only to the treatment of structures in this study. See also David Murphy, "Rationale and Formulation of a Supratypology for Vernacular Houses," in Thomas Carter and Bernard L. Herman, eds., *Perspectives in Vernacular Architecture, III* (Columbia: University of Missouri Press, 1989), 232–33, for an example of a method of typing vernacular structures.

2. When scholars attempt to ascertain Germanic qualities of architecture based only on exterior views of structures, they can conclude that Germans readily adopted American house types and architectural styles. However, a thorough analysis of type, structure, and floor plan is necessary to arrive at a fully informed understanding of how German-Americans creatively adapted to the dominant culture while preserving much of their folk culture.

Scholars have presented various interpretations of tradition vs. assimilation when treating the material culture of German-Americans. Hildegard Binder Johnson, as quoted by Thomas Harvey, claimed, "The Germans could not buck the influence of the Sears Roebuck catalogue and the railroad." And Harvey asserted: "The rejection of German culture is also seen in the architectural styles and building types found in German areas. There are few strikingly German structures in Minnesota." See Thomas Harvey, "A Rejection of Traditional German Forms," in Clarence A. Glasrud, ed., *A Heritage Deferred: The German Americans in Minnesota* (Moorhead, Minn.: Concordia College, 1981), 72–73. Roger Kennedy explained that Germans who settled in the state prior to the 1870s appeared to assimilate readily—or at least did not display any clearly evident German qualities in the designs of their houses. He claims that Germans who immigrated from 1870 to 1895 were, by contrast, less willing to embrace American ways. See Roger Kennedy, *Minnesota Houses: An Architectural and Historical View* (Minneapolis: Dillon Press, 1967), 67–68.

On the other hand, the architectural historian John Fitchen recognizes that: "Tradition in native practices and customs has always been a dominant and very powerful force among peoples and cultures in former times. Innumerable examples come to mind, embracing language and its local dialects, dress and ornament, food and its preparation, social relationships—in fact, all those characteristics of belief and conduct, of attitude and habit, that particularize each human culture and distinguish one tribe or people from another. Building has been no exception. It too has quite universally shown its own adherence to time-honored custom, and even more strongly so, perhaps, because of its constant and highly visible presence." John Fitchen, *Building Construction before Mechanization* (Cambridge, Mass.: MIT Press, 1986), 35.

The present study demonstrates that Germanic qualities of houses in St. John the Baptist parish are revealed in their arrangement and use of interior space.

3. In fig. 4:3a, August and Anna Illies stand on the left side of the porch. Henry Illies's wife, Mary, stands between them and a hired woman, who holds one of the Illies children. Henry stands in front of the porch, on the right. To his right is Math [Matthew] Thomey, the builder of the newly completed house. Lena Mueller, interview by author, Lake Henry, Minn., July 17, 1997.

4. "Century Farms: Held for Generations. Homesteader's Second House Still in Use by Illies Family," *Sauk Centre (Minn.) Herald*, November 10, 1976, 12B.

5. Rev. Paschal Botz, "Botz Family Tree" (manuscript, Collegeville, Minn.: St. John's Abbey, 1986), 1.

6. Nothing remains on parish farms to provide evidence of the stages of growth from the early subsistence-level shelters to the fully appointed dairy farms of the 1890s. Evidence does exist on other German-American farms in the county of various log and stone structures that functioned as predecessors of the dairy barn, chicken coop, swine house, and pump room. See Marilyn Salzi

Brinkman and William Towner Morgan, *Light from the Hearth: Central Minnesota Pioneers and Early Architecture* (St. Cloud, Minn.: North Star Press, 1982), 37–69.

7. See Allen G. Noble, *Wood, Brick and Stone: The North American Settlement Landscape*, vol. 2, *Barns and Farm Structures* (Amherst: University of Massachusetts Press, 1984), 59–60. The frame of the Botz barn is also similar to that of some Pennsylvania barns. See Robert F. Ensminger, *The Pennsylvania Barn: Its Origin, Evolution, and Distribution in North America* (Baltimore, Md.: Johns Hopkins University Press, 1992), 66, 124–25; and Hermann Kaiser and Helmut Ottenjann, "Zur Geschichte des niederdeustchen Hallenhaus" [Toward a History of the Northern German Hallenhaus (House-Barn)], *Museumsdorf Cloppenburg: Niedersächsisches Freilichtmuseum* [Cloppenburg Village Museum: Niedersachsen Open Air Museum] (Cloppenburg, West Germany: Niedersächsisches Freilichtmuseum Verlag, 1988): 109–15.

8. For further discussion of the I-house type in the Upper Midwest, see Fred W. Peterson, "Tradition and Change in Nineteenth-Century Iowa Farmhouses," *Annals of Iowa* 52, no. 3 (summer 1993): 251–81.

9. When the second-generation Imdiekes occupied the house, the family included Bernard, his wife, and their nine children. Henry and Elizabeth Imdieke remained there, as did Elizabeth's mother. A hired man and two nuns completed the household. Dale Imdieke, interview by author, Meire Grove, Minn., August 18, 1988.

10. By adding a lean-to measuring 16 by 56 feet on the north side of the barn during the early 1920s, the Imdiekes created milking stations for sixteen more cows.

11. Al Nietfeld (Arnold's grandson), interview by author, Melrose, Minn., April 3, 1992. The 1891 brick house was the third dwelling to be erected on the farm. The family settled there in 1874 and built a log cabin that they later replaced with a small frame house. Apparently, that structure was a modified balloon frame made from locally milled lumber. Arnold's son Conrad explained that after the house was moved from its original site, he and a neighbor boy took it down piece by piece. He discovered that the studs were rough-sawn boards only 1¼ by 4 inches instead of 2 by 4 inches. He recalled this

detail clearly because he later nailed two of each of these studs together to frame a closet on the second story of the brick house. Conrad Nietfeld, interview by author, Melrose, Minn., April 8, 1992.

12. The attic of the Nietfeld home later became the drying-and-storage area for products of the Nietfeld Seed Company.

13. Frederika Imdieke, interview by author, Meire Grove, Minn., September 15, 1988. The Imdiekes eventually installed a modern hot-air furnace in the room behind the kitchen. One might speculate that the failed heating experiment at the Nietfelds inspired Joseph Imdieke to use a modern manufactured appliance.

14. The elevation and floor plan of the Frank and Elizabeth Deters farmhouse, formerly in Section 2 of Lake George Township, were virtually identical to those of the Haverkamp house. See fig. 5:7.

15. This configuration of interior spaces was, of course, not unique to St. John the Baptist parish. Professionally designed Foursquare houses were sometimes divided into three chambers, with the largest space designated as the living room and the two back rooms serving as kitchen and bedroom. A large fireplace marked the center of the square floor plan. See Gordon=Van Tine Company, *Gordon=Van Tine's Grand Book of Plans for Everybody*, House Plan No. 117 (Davenport, Iowa: Gordon=Van Tine Company, 1910), 29.

16. Food and Recipe File, Heritage Center, Stearns County Historical Society, St. Cloud, Minn.

17. A late-nineteenth-century household book by an anonymous German-American woman in Stearns County bears eloquent testimony to the stamina, resourcefulness, and wide range of knowledge farm wives needed to keep their households well fed and healthy. Some notes and recipes in the book are carefully written in old-script German. The same hand also masterfully wrote in modern English script. In addition to the large-scale recipes, she recorded formulas for "home cures." As chemist, nurse, and housewife, she mixed substances to ease bodily aches and pains or cure a cold, the croup, or cough. One particularly ethnic cure for a cold was, "to a pint of beer take two tablespoons of brown sugar. Boil about five minutes. Take often as much as you like." As technician

and manufacturer, she made her own floor mops, mixed her own floor wax; and as beautician, she used one formula for shampoo and another for hair tonic. Leaving the manufacture of beer to local breweries, she detailed how to make wine from a variety of wild and cultivated fruits and how to create brandy through a long-term process that began with the mixing of blackberries with good rye whiskey. Anonymous manuscript, Food and Recipe File, Heritage Center, Stearns County Historical Society, St. Cloud, Minn.

18. Many of the representative houses found in Steven Martens's study of German-American brick farmhouses in Carver County, Minnesota, have no doorway on their principal facade. Entry is at the kitchen by one or more doors, as it was in the houses discussed here. See Steven Cleo Martens, "Ethnic Tradition and Innovation as Influences on a Rural, Midwestern Building Vernacular: Findings from Investigation of Brick Houses in Carver County, Minnesota" (master's thesis, University of Minnesota, 1988).

19. See Charles Bergengren, "From Lovers to Murderers: The Etiquette of Entry and the Social Implications of House Form," *Winterthur Portfolio* 29, no. 1 (1994): 44–72.

NOTES TO CHAPTER V

1. Concepts and values related to the discussion of space and place in this chapter owe much to the work of the cultural geographer Yi Fu Tuan. See Yi Fu Tuan, *Space and Place: The Perspective of Experience* (Minneapolis: University of Minnesota Press, 1977), and idem, "Place and Culture: Analeptic for Individuality and the World's Indifference," in Wayne Franklin and Michael Steiner, eds., *Mapping American Culture* (Iowa City: University of Iowa Press, 1992), 27–49.

2. In a study of various European nationalities published in 1931, Walter Terpenning characterized German villagers and farmers as "industrious, thrifty, orderly, neat, clean, quiet, peaceful, reliable, religious, sociable, kind, and friendly." While one must take care not to stereotype, this cluster of traits can also be recognized in German-Americans of St. John the Baptist parish. See

Walter A. Terpenning, *Village and Open-Country Neighborhoods* (New York: Century Company, 1931), 159–217.

3. "Keep up Dairying: . . . ," *Melrose (Minn.) Beacon,* January 9, 1903.

4. For a study of a similar German-American Catholic farming community in the Midwest, see Sonya Salamon, "Ethnic Communities and the Structure of Agriculture," *Rural Sociology* 50, no. 3 (1985): 323–40.

5. The local priest preached one sermon in German each Sunday at the Church of St. John the Baptist until 1950. By 1956 the last traces of the language had been removed from the Sunday service because fourth- and fifth-generation parishioners had ceased using the native tongue.

6. See R. Priebsch and W. E. Collinson, *The German Language* (London: Faber and Faber, 1934), 434–47.

7. See John R. Stilgoe, *Common Landscape of America, 1580 to 1845* (New Haven, Conn.: Yale University Press, 1982), 3–29.

8. Original settlement patterns tended to ignore the regularity of the federal-survey parcels of land. Pioneers selected farmsteads from the perspective of their own experience and for qualities of the land as individually perceived, not primarily because of the scale and orientation of the given plat. They arranged these elements of their built environment in a pattern that placed the church at the physical and hence spiritual center of the community.

9. The German anthropologist Anneliese Siebert describes the folk character of Niedersachsen Germans *(der Volkscharacter in Niedersachsen)* as one of quiet and calm persistence *(die ruhige und sichere Beharrung).* She writes that they tend to show mistrust and skepticism toward new developments, reasonably searching for the inner meanings of events rather than focusing on external appearances. Their calm composure enables them to realize ways of doing things that, once established, they will unalterably follow to the point of defiance. As practical people, they are not given to fantasies but instead anchor their two feet on the ground *(bliebt immer mit einem Fusz auf der Erde).* Anneliese Siebert, "Der Baustoff als gestaltender Faktor niedersächsischer Kulterlandschaften: Beitrag zur niedersächsischen Landeskunde und allgemein Kulturgeographie" [Building Materials as a Formative Factor of the Niedersachsen Cultural Landscape: A Contribution to Niedersachsen Regional Studies and General Cultural Geography], in *Forschungen zur Deutschen Landeskunde* (Research for the German Cultural Landscape), Band [vol.] 167 (Bad Godesberg, West Germany: Bundesforchungsantstalt für Landeskunde und Raumordnung Selbstverlag, 1969), 86–87.

10. Building Brick Association of America, *A House of Brick of Moderate Cost* (Boston: Rogers and Manson, 1910), 80–81. Parishioners' appreciation of these qualities of brick was reinforced by their sense of *die Landschaft*—that well-ordered, well-maintained environment in which they labored to preserve well-being.

11. Roger R. Imdieke, "Herman G. Imdieke Biography" (manuscript, St. Cloud, Minn.: Stearns County Historical Society, n.d.), 4.

12. The longtime residents quoted here were between eighty-six and ninety-six years old when I interviewed them.

13. Al Imdieke, interview by author, James City, N.Dak., September 22, 1988.

14. Conrad Nietfeld, interview by author, Melrose, Minn., April 8, 1992.

15. Frederika Imdieke, interview by author, Meire Grove, Minn., September 15, 1988.

16. J. W. Crary, Sr., *Sixty Years a Brickmaker: A Practical Treatise on Brickmaking and Burning* (Indianapolis, Ind.: T. A. Randall, 1890), 71.

17. Local carpenters made the window frames of oak that fit the size and scale of the specific wall opening. The bricks that framed the window were finished in what is called "the king's closure"—a header and stretcher brick placed every other course that ties the brick pattern together at the ends of courses that are interrupted by the window opening. A "queen's closure," which uses a half-brick, creates a slightly more complex pattern. Brickmasons in the parish used the simpler and more direct of the two kinds of closure.

18. Other documented parish brick farmhouses that contain variations on this basic floor plan are: Henry and Elizabeth Wehlage farmhouse (1880–90, first unit of house included kitchen and two back chambers with

central chimney); Arnold Nietfeld farmhouse (1891, west half of first floor [fig. 4:19b]); Frank and Elizabeth Deters farmhouse (ca. 1895, main section of first floor [fig. 5:7]); Henry and Wilhelmina Haverkamp farmhouse (1899, main section of first floor [fig. 3:8b]); Catherine Van Beck farmhouse (1902, first floor similar to Schmiesing floor plan); John and Anna Eibensteiner farmhouse (1904, west half of first floor [fig. 4:22b]); Richard Imdieke farmhouse (1915, first floor [fig. 4:25b] similar to Schmiesing [fig. 4:24b] and Van Beck floor plans).

19. In a study of a village in southwestern Germany, Utz Jeggle notes that "As in the village and its fields, so too in every house there was no free disposition over space. Everything had its place." In the houses, "The division of space was preordained, as was the nature of their furnishings." This kind of strict adherence to traditional building and interior finish seems to be the formative cause for the transfer of a "preordained" floor plan from northwestern Germany to central Minnesota. See Utz Jeggle, "The Rules of the Village: On the Cultural History of the Peasant World in the Last 150 Years," in Richard J. Evans and R. Lee, eds., *The German Peasantry: Conflict and Community in Rural Society from the Eighteenth to the Twentieth Centuries* (London: Croom Helm, 1986), 265–89.

20. It would be misleading and inappropriate to attribute "style" to St. John the Baptist parish brick farmhouses in the same way "styles" are designated for the ornamentation of the Ohio farmhouse. While brick farmhouses in the parish display significant architectural qualities, they comprise a vernacular variety of building that does not employ popular stylistic idioms. See Richard W. Longstreth, "The Problem with 'Style,'" *Forum: Bulletin of the Committee on Preservation of the Society of Architectural Historians* 6 (December 1984).

21. As early as 1880, prospective builders in St. John the Baptist parish who wanted a local example of style and show could study the St. Patrick's Parish House in Melrose. Somewhat more restrained than the western Ohio farmhouse, this building offered most of the decorative flourishes used in Victorian designs—an ornamental porch with balcony, patterned bargeboards, metal cresting on a multigabled roof, bay window, and window shutters. Despite its authority as a unit of the church complex, the parish house was not viewed as an orthodox source of inspiration for new parish homes.

22. A survey of two other areas in the Upper Midwest where German-Americans constructed many brick houses indicates that the isolation of rural communities insulated them from influences from the dominant culture. The brick houses in the vicinity of Watertown, Wisconsin (a larger, commercial city), were built in various nineteenth-century revival styles. Farm families in Carver County, Minnesota, like residents of St. John the Baptist parish, built in a simple vernacular manner that reflected relatively little popular influence. Here again it is worth recalling that St. John the Baptist was an enclave surrounded by other German-American Catholic parishes. See Evelyn Ruddick Rose, *Our Heritage of Homes* (Watertown, Wisc.: Watertown Historical Society, 1980), and Steven Cleo Martens, "Ethnic Tradition and Innovation as Influences on a Rural, Midwestern Building Vernacular: Findings from Investigation of Brick Houses in Carver County, Minnesota" (master's thesis, University of Minnesota, 1988).

NOTES TO CHAPTER VI

1. Certain church-based groups also helped structure parishioners' lives in St. John the Baptist and other nearby parishes. For example, the priest organized families into eight alphabetically ordered groups that were responsible for handling social activities, charity fund-raising, and bazaars. Additionally, there was the Mission Society, which consisted of nine groups of parishioners who met at each others' homes throughout the year to focus on various concerns related to the churches' foreign missionary work. The locus of these activities was the ecclesiastical grounds that held the large brick church, the rectory, and the cemetery. Ronald G. Klietsch, "The Religious Social System of the German-Catholics of the Sauk" (master's thesis, University of Minnesota, 1958), 60–61, 66.

2. Religious and secular education were inextricably related: The district schoolteacher, also known as the

Kirchenväeter (church father), was seminary-trained and guided by the parish priest to include religious training in the standard curriculum. The parochial school built in Meire Grove in 1916 was also designated as a district school. See Paulin Blecker, *Deep Roots: One Hundred Years of Catholic Life in Meire Grove* (St. Cloud, Minn.: Sentinel Publishing, 1958), 83–84.

3. The Verein was a mutual-aid organization that offered monetary assistance to members in good standing who were suffering misfortune and need. The Verein also assisted at funerals of deceased members and sponsored Masses said for the dead. The Christian Mothers Society involved parish women in promoting young people's religious education. It, too, performed mutual-aid functions. And when a member died, others in the organization recited the Rosary at her home during the wake before the funeral.

4. Total devotion to the service of God became possible through the reception of the Sacrament of Holy Orders, whereby one became a priest, or by taking final vows as a monk (brother) or a nun. The large number of parishioners who took this path to grace is evidence of the strength and authenticity of the faith practiced in the home.

5. Editorial staff, Catholic University of America, Washington, D.C., "Sacramentals," *New Catholic Encyclopedia,* (New York: McGraw-Hill, 1967), 12:791.

6. See Francis X. Weiser, *Handbook of Christian Feasts and Customs: The Year of the Lord in Liturgy and Folklore* (New York: Harcourt, Brace and World, 1952), 162–64, for a description of various pre–Christian and Christian water rites that pertain to fertility, good health, and new life.

7. Bede Scholz, "Sacramentals: The Sacramentals in Agriculture," *Orates Frates* 5 (1931): 323.

8. Ibid., 324.

9. Two sources for this service are found in the early history of the Church. The first is a litany that originated in fifth-century Gaul among Christians there who sought God's deliverance from ongoing catastrophes. The second is a litany formally instituted in Rome early in the seventh century by Pope Gregory the Great, in circumstances similar to those that had afflicted Gaul. It is said that, as the Christians confessed their sins and prayed

for each other, the effects of a recent flood and plague abated. This litany was based on a pre–Christian ritual that Romans performed when seeking the protection of the god Robigus (or Robiga) against frost and blight that endangered field crops, especially grains. This ritual may in turn have stemmed from rites the ancient Greeks performed for the gods Demeter and Dionysus (Ceres and Bacchus) in order to ensure good crops.

10. The symbolism of the palms blessed by the Church on Palm Sunday derives from pre–Christian rites in which maidens who were touched by newly sprouting branches of bushes were believed to experience health and fertility. The direct symbolism comes from Christ's triumphal entry into Jerusalem—the first Palm Sunday—during which he was welcomed by crowds waving palms. See Matthew 21:8 and John 12:13.

11. Rev. Herman Rolfus and Rev. F. J. Brändle, *The Means of Grace,* adapted from the German by Rev. Richard Brennan (New York: Benziger Brothers, 1894), 348.

12. Lena Mueller, interview by author, Lake Henry, Minn., July 17, 1997.

13. Rolfus and Brändle, *Means of Grace,* 345–46.

14. Lena Mueller, interview.

15. Rolfus and Brändle, *Means of Grace,* 131–32.

16. Frederika Imdieke, interview by author, Meire Grove, Minn., September 15, 1988. The women made the arches in the yard of the Henry and Elizabeth Imdieke farmhouse, across the street from the church. Women of the congregation routinely gathered at the Imdieke home after Sunday Mass.

17. Weiser, *Handbook of Christian Feasts and Customs,* 265–66.

18. Bishops' Committee on the Liturgy, *Catholic Household Blessings and Prayers* (Washington, D.C.: National Conference of Catholic Bishops, 1988), 155. Although the form of this prayer is in a contemporary idiom, it captures the content of older prayers for the consecration of a new house. The practices of blessing the site, construction, and completed house are indeed of ancient origin and universal practice.

19. Lena Mueller, interview. Prayers offered at home were said in German. Church sermons were given in German, but the Mass was conducted in Latin.

20. See Ann Taves, *The Household of Faith: Roman Catholic*

Devotions in the Mid-Nineteenth Century (Notre Dame, Ind.: University of Notre Dame Press, 1986).

21. Francis Xavier Lusance, *Visits to Jesus in the Tabernacle: Hours and Half-Hours of Adoration before the Blessed Sacrament* (New York: Benziger Brothers, 1898), 479–83.

22. Normal obligations of the family were to attend Sunday Mass throughout the year and participate in nine days of sacramental celebrations performed for the entire parish (i.e., the observance of Holy Week, Rogation Days, the Feast of Corpus Christi, and Christmas). In addition to these occasions, from 1872 until the 1930s the Botz family attended approximately thirty special services of baptism, communion, and weddings that involved their children. Jacob's brother John and his large family lived nearby in the parish, increasing the number of special church services that the extended family attended. Friends and neighbors expected similar participation.

23. Colleen McDannell, "The Home as Sacred Space in American Protestant and Catholic Popular Thought, 1840 to 1900" (Ph.D. diss., Temple University, 1984), 161–62. Father Colman J. Barry claimed that Germans "love the beauty of the church edifice and the pomp of ceremonies, belfries and bells, organs and sacred music, processions, feast days, sodalities, and the most solemn celebrations of First Communion and weddings. These and other like things, although not essential to Catholic faith and life, foster piety and are so dear and sacred to the faithful that not without great danger could they be taken from them." Colman J. Barry, *The Catholic Church and German Americans* (Washington, D.C.: Catholic University of America Press, 1953), 294.

NOTES TO CHAPTER VII

1. Ernst Friedrich Schumacher, *Small Is Beautiful: Economics as If People Mattered* (New York: Harper and Row, 1973).

2. Clifford E. Clark, "Domestic Architecture as an Index to Social History: The Romantic Revival and the Cult of Domesticity in America, 1840–1870," *Journal of Interdisciplinary History* 7 (summer 1976): 33–56.

3. See James A. Montmarquet, *The Idea of Agrarianism:*

From Hunter-Gather to Agrarian Radical in Western Culture (Moscow: University of Idaho Press, 1989), 86–97.

4. Merrill D. Peterson, ed. *The Portable Thomas Jefferson* (New York: Viking Press, 1975), 384.

5. Brooks Atkinson, ed. *The Complete Essays and Other Writings of Ralph Waldo Emerson* (New York: Modern Library, 1940), 749.

6. Ibid., 750.

7. Ibid., 757.

8. Theologians and clerics of churches that have prescribed doctrine have, however, formulated both theory and practice that apply traditional Christian meaning to the life and labors of the farmer. The theory constitutes the essential dogma, doctrine, and sacraments of the Church as they relate to agriculture; the practice involves the liturgies, litanies, and sacramentals of worship that connect the spiritual power of the Church with the physical energies of the land and the manual labor of the farmer. Whether employing the terms *rural synthesis* or *rural piety*, clerics interpret the work of the farmer as the keeper of God's grace that is manifested in the fertility of the land. It is this fertility that is a divine gift to humankind of which the farmer is a steward. See Martin Thorton, *Rural Synthesis: The Religious Basis of Rural Culture* (London: Skeffington and Son, 1961), for this position as expressed by a theologian of the Anglican Church; and Ronald G. Klietsch, "The Religious Social System of the German-Catholics of the Sauk" (master's thesis, University of Minnesota, 1958), for an analysis of a "rural piety" fostered by the Roman Catholic Church.

9. Montmarquet, *The Idea of Agrarianism*, 34–39.

10. Sister Mary Gilbert Kelly, "The Work of Bishop Loras and Father Pierz for Colonization," *Catholic Immigrant Colonization Projects in the United States, 1815–60,* United States Catholic Historical Society Series, no. 17 (New York: United States Catholic Historical Society, 1939), 167.

11. See David W. Noble, *The End of American History: Democracy, Capitalism, and the Metaphor of the Two Worlds in Anglo-American Historical Writing, 1880–1980* (Minneapolis: University of Minnesota Press, 1985);

and Edward N. Saveth, *American Historians and European Immigrants, 1875–1925* (New York: Russel and Russel, 1965). Saveth explains how American historians assented to tenets of Social Darwinism by asserting the superiority of Aryan ancestry. Those who could claim this racial supremacy were descendants of an Anglo-Saxon race. This ancestry could be traced to German as well as English sources. Both branches of this family tree were, however, presented in the most general terms. There was a general failure to understand that Germans or German-speaking peoples represented a wide variety of social orders, political virtues, and religious beliefs.

12. Klietsch, "Religious Social System," 66.

BIBLIOGRAPHY

PRIMARY SOURCES

Beecher, Catharine, and Harriet Beecher Stowe. *The American Woman's Home.* New York: J. B. Ford, 1869.

Bowler, George. *Chapel and Church Architecture with Designs for Parsonages.* Boston: J. P. Jewett, 1856.

Brauns, C. *Praktische Belehrungen und Rathschläge für Reisende und Auswanderer nach Amerika* [Practical Instructions and Advice for Travelers and Emigrants to America]. Braunschweig: Waifenhaus Buchdruckerei, 1829.

Building Brick Association of America. *A House of Brick of Moderate Cost.* Boston: Rogers and Manson, 1910.

Crary, J. W., Sr. *Sixty Years a Brickmaker: A Practical Treatise on Brickmaking and Burning.* Indianapolis, Ind.: T. A. Randall, 1890.

Downing, Alexander Jackson. *The Architecture of Country Houses.* New York: D. Appleton, 1850.

Ekblaw, K. J. T. *Farm Structures.* New York: Macmillan, 1914.

Federal Land Survey field notes. Township 125 North, Range 33 West (Grove Township); Township 125 North, Range 34 West (Getty Township); Township 124 North, Range 33 West (Spring Hill Township). St. Paul: Minnesota Historical Society.

Gaume, Abbe. *Catechism and Perseverance.* Boston: Thomas B. Noonan, 1881.

Gordon=Van Tine Company. *Gordon=Van Tine's Grand Book of Plans for Everybody.* Davenport, Iowa: Gordon=Van Tine Company, 1910.

Halsted, Byron D. *Barn Plans and Outbuildings.* New York: Orange Judd Company, 1890.

Hodgson, Fred T. *Cyclopedia of Bricklaying, Stone Masonry, Concretes, Stuccos and Plasters.* Chicago: Frederick J. Drake, 1913.

Imdieke, Roger R. "Herman G. Imdieke Biography." Manuscript. St. Cloud, Minn.: Stearns County Historical Society, n.d.

Keppers, Albert J., and Erna Keppers. "The Ferdinand H. Eveslage Family History." Manuscript. St. Cloud, Minn.: Stearns County Historical Society, n.d.

Kuefler, Irvin. "Genealogy of the Kuefler Family." Manuscript. Calgary: Alberta, Canada., n.d.

Meire Grove City File, Heritage Center, Stearns County Historical Society, St. Cloud, Minn.

Plat Book of Stearns County, Minnesota, 1896. Philadelphia: Pinkney and Brown, 1896.

Plat Book. Stearns County, Minnesota. St. Paul: Webb Publishing Company, 1925.

Plat Book of Stearns County, Minnesota. Fergus Falls, Minn.: Thomas O. Nelson Company, 1947.

Radford Architectural Company. *The Radford American Homes: 100 House Plans.* Riverside, Ill.: Radford Architectural Company, 1903.

Radford, William A. *Radford's Brick Houses and How to Build Them.* Chicago: Radford Architectural Company, 1912.

Roberts, Isaac Phillips. *The Farmstead: The Making of a Rural Home and the Lay-Out of the Farm.* New York: Macmillan, 1900.

Rolfus, Rev. Herman, and Rev. F. J. Brändle. *The Means of Grace.* Adapted from the German by Rev. Richard Brennan. New York: Benziger Brothers, 1894.

Shadler, F. J. *The Beauties of the Catholic Church.* New York: Fr. Pustet, 1881.

Sholl, Charles. *Working Designs for Ten Catholic Churches, Containing All Dimensions, Details, and Specifications.* New York: D. and J. Sadler, 1869.

Stearns County, Minnesota: Atlas and Plat Book. Battle Lake, Minn.: Accurate Publishing, 1989.

United States manuscript population census schedules, Getty, Grove, Lake George, and Spring Hill Townships, Stearns County, Minnesota, 1870, 1880, 1895, and 1905. St. Paul: Minnesota Historical Society.

INTERVIEWS BY THE AUTHOR

Imdieke, Al. Valley City, N.Dak., September 22, 1988.

Imdieke, Dale. Meire Grove, Minn., October 11, 1983, August 18, 1988, and October 23, 1995.

Imdieke, Frederika. Meire Grove, Minn., September 15, 1988.

Klaphake, Marcia. Meire Grove, Minn., April 27, 1996.

Meyer, Alois "Red." Meire Grove, Minn., October 7, 1994.

Meyer, Florence. Meire Grove, Minn., November 10, 1995, and April 27, 1996.

Michels, Walter and Marion. Villard, Minn., March 22, 1994.

Mueller, Lena. Lake Henry, Minn., July 17, 1997.

Nietfeld, Al. Melrose, Minn., April 3, 1992.

Nietfeld, Conrad. Melrose, Minn., April 8, 1992.

Carl Rheingans, Lac qui Parle County, Minn., September 4, 1984.

SECONDARY SOURCES: BOOKS

Adams, Willi Paul. *The German-Americans: An Ethnic Experience.* Translated and adapted by La Vern J. Rippley and Eberhard Reichmann. Indianapolis, Ind.: Max Kade German-American Center, 1993.

Allen, James Paul, and Eugene James Turner. *We the People: An Atlas of America's Ethnic Diversity.* New York: Macmillan, 1988.

Atkinson, Brooks, ed. *The Complete Essays and Other Writings of Ralph Waldo Emerson.* New York: Modern Library, 1940.

Barry, Colman, J. *The Catholic Church and German Americans.* Washington, D.C.: Catholic University of America, 1953.

Bealer, Alex W. *The Tools That Built America.* New York: Bonanza Books, 1976.

Beals, Carleton. *Brass Knuckle Crusade: The Great Know-Nothing Conspiracy, 1820–60.* New York: Hastings House, 1968.

Benjamin, Steven L., ed. *Occasional Papers of the Society for German-American Studies, No. 10.* Northfield, Minn.: St. Olaf Symposium on German Americana, 1979.

Berger, Peter L. *The Sacred Canopy: Elements of a Sociological Theory of Religion.* New York: Doubleday, 1967.

Bishops' Committee on the Liturgy. *Catholic Household Blessings and Prayers.* Washington, D.C.: National Conference of Catholic Bishops, 1988.

Blecker, Paulin. *Deep Roots: One Hundred Years of Catholic Life in Meire Grove.* St. Cloud, Minn.: Sentinel Publishing, 1958.

Blegen, Theodore C. *Minnesota: A History of the State.* Minneapolis: University of Minnesota Press, 1978.

Borchert, John R. *America's Northern Heartland: An Economic and Historical Geography of the Upper Midwest.* Minneapolis: University of Minnesota Press, 1987.

Botz, Rev. Paschal. "Botz Family Tree." Manuscript. Collegeville, Minn.: St. John's Abbey, 1986.

Brinkman, Marilyn Salzi, and William Towner Morgan. *Light from the Hearth: Central Minnesota Pioneers and Early Architecture.* St. Cloud, Minn.: North Star Press, 1982.

Brinkman, Marilyn, et al. *Bringing Home the Cows: Family Dairy Farming in Stearns County, 1853–1986.* St. Cloud, Minn.: Stearns County Historical Society, 1988.

Brunskill, R. W. *Illustrated Book of Vernacular Architecture.* London: Faber and Faber, 1971.

──────────. *Vernacular Architecture of the Lake Countries.* London: Faber and Faber, 1974.

Centennial 1881–1981, "Heritage of Faith," Sacred Heart Parish, Freeport, Minnesota. Chicago: C. P. D. Corporation, 1981.

Clark, Clifford E., Jr. *The American Family Home, 1800–1960.* Chapel Hill: University of North Carolina Press, 1986.

──────────., ed. *Minnesota in a Century of Change: The State and Its People since 1900.* St. Paul: Minnesota Historical Society Press, 1989.

Cohen, David Steven. *The Dutch-American Farm.* New York: New York University Press, 1992.

Conzen, Kathleen Neils. *Making Their Own America: Assimilation Theory and the German Peasant Pioneer.* New York: Berg, 1990.

Davey, Norman. *A History of Building Materials.* London: Phoenix House, 1961.

Dickinson, Robert E. *The Regions of Germany.* New York: Oxford University Press, 1945.

Dues, Greg. *Catholic Customs and Traditions: A Popular Guide.* Mystic, Conn.: Twenty-third Publications, 1989.

Editorial staff, Catholic University of America, Washington, D.C. *New Catholic Encyclopedia.* "Confession" 4, "Medals" 9, "Novena" 10, "Rosary" 12, "Sacramentals" 12. New York: McGraw-Hill, 1967.

Eliade, Mircea. *The Sacred and the Profane: The Nature of Religion.* New York: Harcourt, Brace and World, 1957.

Ensminger, Robert F. *The Pennsylvania Barn: Its Origin, Evolution, and Distribution in North America.* Baltimore, Md.: Johns Hopkins University Press, 1992.

Fell, Marie L. *The Foundations of Nativism in American Textbooks, 1833–1860*. Washington, D.C.: University of America Press, 1945.

Fiedler, Alfred, and Jochen Helbig. *Bauernhaus in Sachsen* [Farmhouses in Saxony]. Berlin: Akademie Verlag, 1967.

Fitchen, John. *The New World Dutch Barn*. Syracuse, N.Y.: Syracuse University Press, 1968.

_____. *Building Construction before Mechanization*. Cambridge, Mass.: MIT Press, 1986.

Franklin, Wayne, and Michael Steiner, eds. *Mapping American Culture*. Iowa City: University of Iowa Press, 1992.

Fuller, Wayne E. *R.F.D.: The Changing Face of Rural America*. Bloomington: University of Indiana Press, 1964.

Furer, Howard B., ed. *The Germans in America, 1607–1970*. Dobbs Ferry, N.Y.: Oceana Publications, 1973.

Garvan, Beatrice B., and Charles F. Hummel. *The Pennsylvania Germans: A Celebration of Their Arts, 1683–1850*. exh. cat. Philadelphia: Philadelphia Museum of Art; and Winterthur, Del.: Henry Francis du Pont Winterthur Museum, 1982.

Gemeinde Holdorf. *Gemeindechronik Holdorf, 1188–1988* [History of the Village of Holdorf, 1188–1988]. Vechta, West Germany: Vechtaer Druckerei und Verlag, 1988.

Glasrud, Clarence A., ed. *A Heritage Deferred: The German Americans in Minnesota*. Moorhead, Minn.: Concordia College, 1981.

Gleason, Philip. *The Conservative Reformers: German-American Catholics and the Social Order*. Notre Dame, Ind.: University of Notre Dame Press, 1968.

Goodman, David. *From Peasant to Proletarian: Capitalist Developments and Agrarian Transitions*. New York: St. Martin's Press, 1982.

Gordon, Milton M. *Assimilation in American Life: The Role of Race, Religion, and National Origins*. New York: Oxford University Press, 1964.

Grebe, Wilhelm. *Handbuch für das Bauren auf dem Lande* [Handbook for Farmers on the Land]. Berlin: Reichsnahrstandsverlag, 1943.

Gross, Stephen John. "Family and Social Structure in a German-American Community: Munson Township Minnesota, 1856–1900." Master's thesis, University of Minnesota, 1988.

Grow, Lawrence. *The Old House Book of Classic Country Houses: Plans for Traditional American Dwellings*. New York: Sterling Publishing, 1990.

Growth from Deep Roots: St. John the Baptist Church, Meire Grove, Minnesota, 1858–1983. Melrose, Minn.: Lovelace Studio, 1983.

Gruber, Otto. *Bauernhäuser am Bodensee* [Farmers' Houses at Bodensee]. Konstanz und Lindau, West Germany: Jan Thorbecke, 1961.

Gueranger, Abbott. *Paschal Time*. Vol. 3 of *The Liturgical Year*. New York: Benziger Brothers, 1904.

Gulliford, Andrew. *America's Country Schools*. Washington, D.C.: Preservation Press, 1984.

Gurcke, Karl. *Bricks and Brickmaking: A Handbook for Historical Archeology*. Moscow: University of Idaho Press, 1988.

Henny, Rev. P. *The Liturgical Year*. Milwaukee, Wisc.: Bruce Publishing, 1938.

Higham, John. *From Boundlessness to Consolidation: The Transformation of American Culture, 1848–1860*. Ann Arbor: University of Michigan Press, 1969.

Holmquist, June D., ed. *They Chose Minnesota: A Survey of the State's Ethnic Groups*. St. Paul: Minnesota Historical Society Press, 1981.

Huck, Gabe. *A Book of Family Prayers*. New York: Seabury Press, 1979.

Iverson, Noel. *Germania, U.S.A.: Social Change in New Ulm, Minnesota*. Minneapolis: University of Minnesota Press, 1966.

Inoki, Takenori. *Aspects of German Peasant Emigration to the United States, 1815–1914: A Reexamination of Some Behavioral Hypotheses in Migration Theory*. New York: Arno Press, 1981.

Jackson, John Brinkerhoff. *American Space: The Centennial Years, 1865–1876*. New York: W. W. Norton, 1972.

Jordan, Terry G. *German Seed in Texas Soil: Immigrant Farmers in Nineteenth-Century Texas*. Austin: University of Texas Press, 1966.

_____. *American Log Buildings: An Old World Heritage*. Chapel Hill: University of North Carolina Press, 1985.

_____. *The European Culture Area: A Systematic Geography*. New York: Harper and Row, 1988.

Kaiser, Hermann, and Helmut Ottenjann. *Museumsdorf Cloppenburg: Niedersächsisches Freilichtmuseum* [Cloppenburg Village Museum: Niedersächsen Open Air Museum]. Cloppenburg, West Germany:

Museumsdorf Cloppenburg Niedersächsisches
Freilichtmuseum Verlag, 1988.

Kamphoefner, Walter D. *The Westfalians: From Germany to
Missouri.* Princeton, N.J.: Princeton University Press,
1987.

_____, Wolfgang Helbich, and Ulrike Sommer, eds.
*News from the Land of Freedom: German Immigrants
Write Home.* Ithaca, N.Y.: Cornell University Press,
1991.

Kelly, Sister Mary Gilbert. *Catholic Immigrant Colonization
Projects in the United States, 1815–60.* United States
Catholic Historical Society Series, no. 17. New York:
United States Catholic Historical Society, 1939.

Kennedy, Maurice B. *The Complete Rosary.* Chicago: Ziff-
Davis, 1947.

Kennedy, Roger. *Minnesota Houses: An Architectural and
Historical View.* Minneapolis: Dillon Press, 1967.

Klein, Maury. *The Flowering of the Third America: The
Making of an Organizational Society, 1850–1920.*
Chicago: Ivan R. Dee, 1993.

Klietsch, Ronald G. "The Religious Social System of the
German-Catholics of the Sauk." Master's thesis,
University of Minnesota, 1958.

Krause, Herbert. *The Thresher.* Indianapolis, Ind.: Bobbs-
Merrill, 1946.

Langer, William L. *The Revolutions of 1848: Chapters from
Political and Social Upheaval.* New York: Harper and
Row, 1969.

Leonard, Ira M., and Robert D. Parmet. *American Nativism,
1830–1860.* New York: Van Norstrand, 1971.

Lucassen, Jan, and Leo Lucassen, eds. *Migration, Migration
History, History: Old Paradigms and New Perspectives.*
Bern: Peter Lang, 1997.

Luebke, Frederick C., ed. *Ethnicity on the Great Plains.*
Lincoln: University of Nebraska Press, 1980.

Lusance, Francis Xavier. *Visits to Jesus in the Tabernacle:
Hours and Half-Hours of Adoration before the Blessed
Sacrament.* New York: Benziger Brothers, 1898.

_____. *Germans in the New World: Essays in the
History of Immigration.* Urbana: University of Illinois
Press, 1990.

Martens, Steven Cleo. "Ethnic Tradition and Innovation as
Influences on a Rural, Midwestern Building
Vernacular: Findings from Investigation of Brick

Houses in Carver County, Minnesota." Master's thesis,
University of Minnesota, 1988.

McAvoy, Thomas, ed. *Roman Catholicism and the American
Way.* Notre Dame, Ind.: University of Notre Dame
Press, 1960.

Mitchell, William Bell. *The History of Stearns County,
Minnesota.* 2 vols. Chicago: H. C. Cooper, Jr., 1915.

Moltmann, Gunther, ed. *Germans to America: 300 Years of
Immigration, 1683 to 1983.* Stuttgart, West Germany:
Institute for Foreign Cultural Relations in cooperation
with Inter Nationes, Bonn-Bad Godesburg, 1982.

Montmarquet, James A. *The Idea of Agrarianism: From
Hunter-Gatherer to Agrarian Radical in Western Culture.*
Moscow: University of Idaho Press, 1989.

Moser, Lawrence E. *Home Celebrations: Studies in American
Pastoral Liturgy.* Paramus, N.J.: Paulist Press, 1970.

Noble, Allen G. *Wood, Brick and Stone: The North American
Settlement Landscape.* 2 vols. Amherst: University of
Massachusetts Press, 1984.

_____, and Hubert G. H. Wilhelm. *Barns of the
Midwest.* Athens: University of Ohio Press, 1995.

Noble, David W. *The End of American History: Democracy,
Capitalism, and the Metaphor of Two Worlds in Anglo-
American Historical Writing, 1880–1980.* Minneapolis:
University of Minnesota Press, 1985.

O'Conner, Richard. *The German-Americans.* New York:
Little, Brown, 1968.

Perin, Constance. *Everything in Its Place: Social Order and
Land Use in America.* Princeton, N.J.: Princeton
University Press, 1977.

Peterson, Fred W. *Homes in the Heartland: Balloon Frame
Farmhouses of the Upper Midwest, 1850–1920.* Lawrence:
University Press of Kansas, 1992.

Peterson, Merrill D., ed. *The Portable Thomas Jefferson.* New
York: Viking Press, 1975.

Priebsch, R., and W. E. Collinson. *The German Language.*
London: Faber and Faber, 1934.

Rach, Hans-Jurgen. *Bauernhaus, Landarbeiterkaten und
Schitterkaserne* [Farmhouse Types, Farm Labor, and
Crop Storage]. Berlin: Akademie-Verlag, 1974.

Radig, Werner. *Das Bauernhaus in Brandenburg und
Mittebgebiet* [The Farmhouse in Brandenburg and
Meittebgebiet]. Berlin: Akademie-Verlag, 1966.

Rasmussen, Wayne D., ed. *Agriculture in the United States:*

A Documentary History. 4 vols. New York: Random House, 1975.

Redfield, Robert. *The Little Community and Peasant Society and Culture*. Chicago: University of Chicago Press, 1956.

Reese, John B. *Some Pioneers and Pilgrims on the Prairies of Dakota*. Mitchell, S.Dak.: Author, 1920.

Rippley, La Vern J. *The German Americans*. Boston: Twayne, 1976.

Rockwell, Peter. *The Art of Stoneworking: A Reference Guide*. Cambridge, England: Cambridge University Press, 1993.

Rose, Evelyn Ruddick. *Our Heritage of Homes*. Watertown, Wisc.: Watertown Historical Society, 1980.

Rothan, Emmet H. *The German Catholic Immigrant in the United States, 1830–1860*. Washington, D.C.: Catholic University Press, 1946.

Rozycki, Anthony T. "The Evolution of the Hamlets of Stearns County, Minnesota." Master's thesis, University of Minnesota, 1977.

Rudolf, Ferdinand. *Der Rosenkranz des Priesters: Ein Mittel zu seiner Heiligung* [The Priest's Rosary: A Center to His Holiness]. Freiburg im Breisgau, Germany: Herdersche Verlagshandlung, 1911.

Ryden, Kent C. *Mapping the Invisible Landscape: Folklore, Writing, and the Sense of Place*. Iowa City: University of Iowa Press, 1993.

Sale, Randall D., and Edwin D. Karn. *American Expansion: A Book of Maps*. Lincoln: University of Nebraska Press, 1979.

Saveth, Edward N. *American Historians and European Immigrants, 1875–1925*. New York: Russel and Russel, 1965.

Schlebecker, John T. *A History of American Dairying*. Chicago: Rand McNally, 1967.

_____. *Whereby We Thrive: A History of American Farming, 1607–1972*. Ames: Iowa State University Press, 1975.

Schroeder, Adolph E., and Carla Schulz-Geisberg. *Hold Dear as Always: Jette, A German Immigrant Life in Letters*. Columbia: University of Missouri Press, 1988.

Schumacher, Ernst Friedrich. *Small Is Beautiful: Economics as If People Mattered*. New York: Harper and Row, 1973.

Schute, Ursula Maria. *Alte Bürgerhäuser zwischen Weser und Ems* [Old City Houses between the Weser and the Ems]. Hildesheim, West Germany: Verlag Gerstenberg, 1981.

Shannon, Fred A. *The Farmer's Last Frontier: Agriculture, 1860–1897*. Vol 5 of *The Economic History of the United States*. New York: Holt, Rinehart and Winston, 1963.

Shannon, James P. *Catholic Colonization on the Western Frontier*. New Haven, Conn.: Yale University Press, 1957.

Shils, Edward. *Tradition*. Chicago: University of Chicago Press, 1981.

Sigfried, Andre. *America Comes of Age*. Translated by Margaret Ledersert. New York: Harcourt, Brace and Company, 1955.

Smith Marvanna S., comp. *Chronological Landmarks in American Agriculture*. Washington, D.C.: U.S.D.A. Agriculture Information Bulletin no. 425, 1979.

Stanton, Phoebe. *The Gothic Revival and American Church Architecture: An Episode in Taste, 1840–1856*. Baltimore, Md.: Johns Hopkins University Press, 1968.

Stearns, Peter N. *1848: The Revolutionary Tide in Europe*. New York: W. W. Norton, 1974.

Stein, Rudolph. *Bremer Barock und Rokoko* [Baroque and Rococo in Bremen]. Bremen, West Germany: Verlag H. M. Hauschild, 1960.

_____. *Dorfkirchen und Bauernhäuser im Bremer Lande* [Village Churches and Farmhouses in Bremen]. Bremen, West Germany: Verlag H. M. Hauschild, 1967.

Stilgoe, John R. *Common Landscape of America, 1580 to 1845*. New Haven, Conn.: Yale University Press, 1982.

Stille, Ulrich. *Dome, Kirchen, und Kloster in Niedersacshen* [Cathedrals, Churches, and Cloisters in Niedersachsen]. Frankfort am Main, West Germany: W. Weidlich, 1963.

Sullivan, Rev. John F. *The Externals of the Catholic Church: Her Government, Ceremonies, Festivals, Sacramentals, and Devotions*. New York: P. J. Kennedy and Sons, 1918.

Terpenning, Walter A. *Village and Open-Country Neighborhoods*. New York: Century Company, 1931.

Thorton, Martin. *Rural Synthesis: The Religious Basis of Rural Culture*. London: Skeffington and Son, 1961.

Tipton, Frank B. *Regional Variations in the Economic Development of Germany during the Nineteenth Century*. Middletown, Conn.: Wesleyan University Press, 1976.

Tuan, Yi-Fu. *Space and Place: The Perspective of Experience.* Minneapolis: University of Minnesota Press, 1977.

Van Ravensway, Charles. *The Arts and Architecture of German Settlements in Missouri.* Columbia: University of Missouri Press, 1977.

Verband Deutsches Architekten und Ingenieurverien. *Das Bauernhaus im Deutschen Reiche und in seinen Grenzgebieten* [Organization of German Architects and Engineers: The Farmhouse in the German Realm and Its Borders]. Hanover, Germany: Curt R. Vinventz Verlag, 1906.

Walker, Mack. *Germany and the Emigration, 1816–1885.* Cambridge, Mass.: Harvard University Press, 1964.

Weiser, Francis X. *Handbook of Christian Feasts and Customs: The Year of the Lord in Liturgy and Folklore.* New York: Harcourt, Brace and World, 1952.

Wheeley, Thomas C., ed. *The Immigrant Experience: The Anguish of Becoming American.* New York: Dial Press, 1971.

Yzermans, Vincent A. *The Mel and the Rose.* Melrose, Minn.: Melrose Historical Society, 1992.

Zucker, Paul. *Town and Square from the Agora to the Village Green.* New York: Columbia University Press, 1959.

SECONDARY SOURCES: ARTICLES

Bergengren, Charles. "From Lovers to Murderers: The Etiquette of Entry and the Social Implications of House Form." *Winterthur Portfolio* 29, no. 1 (1994): 42–72.

"Century Farms: Held for Generations. Homesteader's Second House Still in Use by Illies Family." *Sauk Centre (Minn.) Herald,* November 10, 1976, 12B.

Clark, Clifford E. "Domestic Architecture as an Index to Social History: The Romantic Revival and the Cult of Domesticity in America, 1840–1870." *Journal of Interdisciplinary History* 7 (summer 1976): 33–56.

Coggeshall, Jon M. "'One of Those Intangibles': The Manifestation of Ethnic Identity in Southwestern Illinois." *Journal of American Folklore* 99 (April–June 1986): 177–207.

Conzen, Kathleen Neils. "The Paradox of German-American Assimilation." In *Occasional Papers of the Society of German-American Studies No. 10,* edited by Steven M. Benjamin, 1–18. Northfield, Minn.: St. Olaf Symposium on German Americana, 1979.

_____. "Immigrants, Immigrant Neighborhoods, and Ethnic Identity." *Journal of American History* 66, no. 3 (December 1979): 603–16.

_____. "Historical Approaches to the Study of Rural Ethnic Communities." In *Ethnicity on the Great Plains,* edited by Frederick C. Luebke, 1–18. Lincoln: University of Nebraska Press, 1980.

_____. "Peasant Pioneers: Generation Succession among German Farmers in Frontier Minnesota." In *The Countryside in the Age of Capitalist Transformation,* edited by Steven Hahn and Jonathan Prude, 259–92. Chapel Hill: University of North Carolina Press, 1985.

Crouch, David. "Representing Ourselves in the Landscape: Cultural Meanings in Everyday Landscape." In *Continuities in Popular Culture: The Present in the Past and the Past in the Present and Future,* edited by Ray B. Browne and Ronald J. Ambrosetti, 26–48. Bowling Green, Ohio: Bowling Green State University Popular Press, 1993.

Dockendorf, Thomas P. "Upper Mississippi Valley Landscape: A Legacy of German Catholic Settlement in Central Minnesota." *Pioneer America Society Transactions* 8 (1985): 85–90.

Duden, Gottfrieds. "Gottfrieds Duden's Report." *Missouri Historical Review* 12 (1917): 1–21; 13 (1918): 251–21; 14 (1919): 29–73.

Glassie, Henry. "Artifact and Culture, Architecture and Society." In *American Material Culture and Folklife,* edited by Simon J. Bonner, 47–62. Ann Arbor, Mich.: UMI Research Press, 1985.

Grout. F. F. "Minnesota Building Brick and Tile." *University of Minnesota Geological Survey, Summary Report No. 2.* George M. Schwartz, dir. (April 1947).

Harevan, Tamara K. "The Home and Family in Historical Perspective." *Social Research* 58 (spring 1991): 253–85.

Heberle, Rudolf. "The Application of Fundamental Concepts in Rural Community Studies." *Rural Sociology* 6 (1941): 203–15.

Henretta, James A. "Families and Farms: Mentalité in Pre-Industrial America." *William and Mary Quarterly* 35 (January 1978): 3–32.

Hummon, David M. "House, Home, and Identity in Contemporary American Culture." In *Housing, Culture, and Design: A Comparative Perspective,* edited by Setha M. Low and Erve Chambers, 207–28. Philadelphia: University of Pennsylvania Press, 1989.

Jeggle, Utz. "The Rules of the Village: On the Cultural History of the Peasant World in the Last 150 Years." In *The German Peasantry: Conflict and Community in Rural Society from the Eighteenth to the Twentieth Centuries,* edited by Richard J. Evans and R. Lee, 265–89. London: Croom Helm, 1986.

Johnson, Hildegard Binder. "Factors Influencing the Distribution of the German Pioneer Population in Minnesota." *Agricultural History* 19 (January 1945): 39–57.

_____. "The Location of German Immigrants in the Middle West." *Annals of the Association of American Geographers* 41, no. 1 (March 1951): 1–41.

Kahn, Clyde F. "The Use of Aerial Photographs in the Geographic Analysis of Rural Settlements." *Photogrammetric Engineering* 17 (1951): 759–71.

Kniffen, Fred B. "Folk Housing: Key to Diffusion." *Annals of the Association of American Geographers* 55 (December 1965): 549–77.

_____, and Henry Glassie. "Building in Wood in the Eastern United States: A Time-Place Perspective." *Geographical Review* 56 (1966): 40–66.

Knobel, Dale T. "'Hans' and the Historian: Ethnic Stereotypes in American Popular Culture, 1820–1860." In *Occasional Papers of the Society of German-American Studies No. 10,* edited by Steven M. Benjamin, 1–18. Northfield, Minn.: St. Olaf Symposium on German Americana, 1979.

Lang, Elfrieda. "Some Characteristics of German Immigrants in Dubois County, Indiana." *Indiana Magazine of History* 42 (1946): 29–46.

Letner, Henry. "'Home . . .': What It Means to a Minnesota Junior Dairyman." *The Kraftsman* 2 (summer 1953): unpaginated.

Lingeman, Richard. "Space and Place: Village and Town." In *The Encyclopedia of American Social History,* edited by Mary Kapiec Cayton, et al, 1249–58. vol. 2. New York: Charles Scribner's Sons, 1993.

Longstreth, Richard W. "The Problem with 'Style'." *Forum:*

Bulletin of the Committee on Preservation of the Society of Architectural Historians 6 (December 1984).

Marshall, Howard Wright. "A Good Gridiron: The Vernacular Design of a Western Cow Town." In *Perspectives in Vernacular Architecture II,* edited by Camille Wells, 81–88. Columbia: University of Missouri Press, 1986.

McAvoy, Thomas. "The Formation of the Catholic Minority in the United States." *Review of Politics* 10, no. 1 (1948): 13–34.

McGrath, Thomas L. "Notes on the Manufacture of Hand-made Bricks." *Bulletin of the Association of Preservation Technology* 11 (1979): 89–95.

Murphy, David. "Rationale and Formulation of a Supratypology for Vernacular Houses." In *Perspectives in Vernacular Architecture, III,* edited by Thomas Carter and Bernard L. Herman, 232–33. Columbia: University of Missouri Press, 1989.

Oliver, Paul. "On the Attributes of Tradition." In *Dwellings, Settlements and Traditions,* edited by Jean-Paul Bourdier and Nezar Alsayyad, 27–34. Lanham, Md.: University Press of America, 1989.

Ostergren, Robert. "The Immigrant Church as a Symbol of Community and Place in the Upper Midwest." *Great Plains Quarterly* (fall 1981): 225–38.

Oszusik, Philippe. "German Influence upon the Architecture of Davenport, Iowa." *Pioneer America Society Transactions* 10 (1987): 17–27.

Peterson, David. "'From Bone Depth': German-American Communities in Rural Minnesota before the Great War." *Journal of American Ethnic History* 11 (winter 1992): 27–55.

Peterson, Fred W. "Vernacular Building and Victorian Architecture: Midwestern American Farm Homes." *Journal of Interdisciplinary History* 12 (winter 1981): 409–27.

_____. "Tradition and Change in Nineteenth-Century Iowa Farmhouses." *Annals of Iowa* 52, no. 3 (summer 1993): 251–81.

Roeber, A. G. "Ethnic and Racial Subcultures: German Speakers." In *The Encyclopedia of American Social History,* edited by Mary Kapiec Cayton, et al, 719–27. vol. 2. New York: Charles Scribner's Sons, 1993.

Salamon, Sonya. "Ethnic Communities and the Structure of

Agriculture." *Rural Sociology* 50, no. 3 (1985): 323–40.

Sanderson, Dwight. "The Rural Community in the United States as an Elementary Group." *Rural Sociology* 1 (1936): 1242–50.

Scholz, Bede. "Sacramentals: The Sacramentals in Agriculture." *Orates Frates* 5 (1931): 323–26.

Siebert, Anneliese. "Der Baustoff als gestaltender Faktor niedersächsischer Kulterlandschaften: Beitrag zur niedersächsischen Landeskunde und allgemein Kulturgeographie" [Building Materials as a Formative Factor of the Niedersachsen Cultural Landscape: A Contribution to Niedersachsen Regional Studies and General Cultural Geography]. In *Forschungen zur Deutschen Landeskunde* [Research for the German Cultural Landscape], 1–249. Band [vol.] 167 (Bad Godesberg, West Germany: Bundesforchungsantstalt für Landeskunde und Raumordnung Selbstverlag, 1969).

Smith, Timothy L. "Religious Denominations as Ethnic Communities: A Regional Case Study." *Church History* 35 (June 1966): unpaginated.

Stanislawski, Dan. "The Origin and Spread of the Grid Pattern Town." *Geographical Review* 36 (January 1943): 105–20.

Tegedar, Vincent. "The Benedictines in Frontier America." *Minnesota History* 32, no. 1 (1951): 34–43.

Thernstrom, Stephen. "Germans" and "Germans from Russia." In *The Harvard Encyclopedia of American Ethnic Groups*, 405–35. Cambridge, Mass.: Harvard University Press, 1980.

Tishler, William, and Christopher S. Witmer. "The Housebarns of East-Central Wisconsin." In *Perspectives in Vernacular Architecture, 11*, edited by Camille Wells, 102–10. Columbia: University of Missouri Press, 1986.

Tuan, Yi-Fu. "Traditional: What Does It Mean?" In *Dwellings, Settlements and Traditions*, edited by Jean-Paul Bourdier and Nezar Alsayyad, 27–34. Lanham, Md.: University Press of America, 1989.

_____. "Place and Culture: Analeptic for Individuality and the World's Indifference." In *Mapping American Culture*, edited by Wayne Franklin and Michael Steiner, 27–49. Iowa City: University of Iowa Press, 1992.

Tweton, D. Jerome. "The Golden Age of Agriculture, 1897–1917." *North Dakota History* 37 (winter 1970): 41–55.

Van Ravensway, Charles. "Missouri River German Settlements. Part I: The Buildings, 1831–1870." *The Magazine Antiques* 63 (January 1978): 178–91.

Vlach, John M. "Form and House Types in American Folk Architecture." In *Introduction to Folklore*, edited by Robert J. Adams, 116–31. Columbus, Ohio: Collegiate Publishing, 1973.

Voegler, Inholf. "The Roman Catholic Culture Region of Western Minnesota." *Pioneer America* 8, no. 2 (1976): 71–83.

Vogt, E. Z., Jr. "Social Stratification in the Rural Midwest: A Structural Analysis." *Rural Sociology* 12 (1947): 364–75.

Walters, William D., Jr. "Nineteenth Century Midwestern Brick." *Pioneer America* 14, no. 3 (1982): 123–36.

Wilhelm, Hubert G. H. "Germans in Ohio." In *To Build in a New Land: Ethnic Landscapes in North America*, edited by Allen G. Noble, 60–78. Baltimore, Md.: Johns Hopkins University Press, 1992.

Wright, Gwendolyn. "Prescribing the Model Home." *Social Research* 58 (spring 1991): 213–25.

INDEX

Meire Grove Cooperative Dairy Association, 20–22, *21*, 58

Melrose, railroad station, 18, 20, 22, 41, 43

Mennonites, emigrate to Pennsylvania, 11

Meyer, Clemens, general store, *57*

Meyer, Daniel, farm, *62*

Meyer, Elizabeth, 9, 15

Meyer, Henry and Elizabeth, 9, 14–15; marriage, 15; farm, 22; land owned, 27; dugout, 33; log cabin, 34–35; church on tract, 39; farmhouse, 46–47, *47*, 177n1

Meyer, Herman and Bernadine, 9, 14–15; marriage, 15; dugout, 33

Meyer, Herman S., raises cattle, 20

Meyer, John Henry, 14–15

Meyer, Joseph, farmstead, 127

Minnesota River, German settlement along, 11

Minnesota Territory, German settlement, 11; created, 13

Mission Society, 181n1

Mississippi River, German settlement along, 11

Montgomery Ward, house catalogs, 47

Mortar joints, finishes, 135, *135*

N

Nelson, Daniel, farmhouse, 99, *100*, *101*

New Ulm, German Catholic parish, 13

New Vienna, Iowa, German Catholic community, 15

Nicollet County, German settlement, 11

Niedersachsen culture, 137, 161. *See also Pfostenwohnhäuser*

Nietfeld, Arnold, farmhouse, 106–9, *108*, *109*, 111, *134*, *135*, 177n1, 178n11

Nietfeld, Conrad, farmhouse, 130

Norwegians, 138, 140–41

O

Oats, harvested, 16–17

Otte, B. H., farmhouse, 177n1

P

Pallauch, J. B., farmhouse, 177n1

Palm Sunday, 149

Panic of *1873*, 18

Patriarchal authority, 27

Penance, sacrament, 147

Penn, William, 11

Pfeffer, Carl, farmer, 18

Pfostenwohnhäuser, 38, *38*, 40, 45, 88–89, 116, 137, 165, 173n20

Pièce sur pièce, building technique, 39–40, *39*

Pierz, Franz, priest, 13–14, 15, 167

Plaques, name-date, 137, *137*

Potatoes, planted, 15

Prayers, priest-led, 149, 153; daily devotions, 154–55

Preemption Act of *1841*, 1, 34

Priests, administer sacraments, 147–50, 152–53, 165; bless objects, 154

Primus, John, farmer, 18

Proverbs, *see* German language

Q

Quaal, Lars L., farmhouse, 140–41, *140*

Quade, Herman, farmhouse, 177n1

Quakers, emigrate to Pennsylvania, 11

R

Radford Architectural Company, 176n27, 176n34

Railroads, transport grain, 18, 19; transport dairy products, 20–21, 22; proposed route through Meire Grove, 28; transport building materials, 41, 43

Rheingans, Carl, 176n33

Rocky Mountain locusts, *see* Grasshoppers

Rogation Days, rituals, 53, 148–49, 153, 156

Rosary beads, 154

Rural piety, 145, 183n8

S

St. Augusta, church, *146*, *151*

St. Augustine, author, 166

St. Cloud, *see* Diocese of St. Cloud

St. Isadore, mass, 149

St. John the Baptist parish, 9; described, 2, 4, 5–6, 29; identity, 23; map, *24;* character traits of parishioners, 125, 126–29, 137, 162–63; as German-American enclave, 161. *See also* Church of St. John the Baptist

St. John's Abbey, established, 14

ILLUSTRATION CREDITS

Except as noted below, the photographs and drawings in this book are by the author.

The following illustrations appear through the courtesy of the institutions or individuals listed:

Akademie-Verlag, Berlin: 108 (top), 137 (top). Originally published in Hans-Jurgen Rach, *Bauernhaus, Landarbeiterkaten und Schitterkaserne* (Berlin: Akademie-Verlag, 1974).

Museumsdorf Cloppenburg, Niedersächsisches Freilichtmuseum, Cloppenburg, Germany: 36, 119, 123.

Verlag H. M. Hauschild, Bremen, Germany: 107. Originally published in Rudolph Stein, *Bremer Barock und Rokoko* (Bremen, West Germany: Verlag H. M. Hauschild, 1967).

Dennis Illies: 88.

Dale Imdieke: 102, 164.

Melrose Area Historical Society, Melrose, Minnesota: cover inset, title-page inset, 37, 42, 46, 50, 52, 53, 57, 67, 68, 75 (bottom), 83.

Minnesota Historical Society, St. Paul: 140.

Nelson Pioneer Farm, Oskaloosa, Iowa: 100

Stearns County Historical Society, St. Cloud, Minnesota: cover, title page, 70 (top), 96, 126, 138, 146, 151, 167.

Vechtaer Druckerei und Verlag, Vechta, Germany: 38 (bottom), 59. Originally published in Gemeinde Holdorf, *Gemeindechronik Holdorf, 1188–1988* (Vechta, West Germany: Vechtaer Druckerei und Verlag, 1988).

Illustrations from the following additional sources:

Paulin Blecker, *Deep Roots: One Hundred Years of Catholic Life in Meire Grove* (St. Cloud: Minn.: Sentinel Publishing, 1958): 7, 21, 23, 35, 40, 159, 165.

Andrew Jackson Downing, *The Architecture of Country Houses* (New York: D. Appleton, 1850): 87, 163.

Honor-Bilt Modern Homes (Chicago: Sears, Roebuck and Company, 1911): 114.

Plat Book of Stearns County, Minnesota, 1896 (Philadelphia: Pinkney and Brown, 1896): 61.

Rev. Herman Rolfus and Rev. F. J. Brändle, *The Means of Grace*. Adapted from the German by Rev. Richard Brennan (New York: Benziger Brothers, 1894): 143, 147, 149, 150.

Verband Deutsches Architekten und Ingenieurverein, *Das Bauernhaus im Deutschen Reiche und in seinen Grenzgebieten* (Hanover, Germany: Curt R. Vinventz Verlag, 1906): 97, 137 (middle).

Maps by Mui D. Le and Alan J. Willis, CartoGraphics Incorporated, Minneapolis: 10, 12, 24, 86.

COLOPHON

Designed and typset by Nora Koch, Gravel Pit Publications.
Composed in Caslon typefaces with Charlemagne display
    type on QuarkXpress 3.32 for Macintosh.
Printed on 6olb. Finch Opaque paper and bound by
    Edwards Brothers, Incorporated, Ann Arbor,
    Michigan.

www.ingramcontent.com/pod-product-compliance
Lightning Source LLC
Jackson TN
JSHW052007131224
75386JS00036B/1222